6 Breakthroughs
to Playing
Bigger in
Leadership,
Business,
and **Life.**

JUSTIN PATTON

praise for BOLD NEW YOU

"In a world where authenticity is often buried in messages of who and what we should be, Justin Patton reminds us that to play bigger you must find a way to reconnect with your own authenticity. This is not a book that offers a one-size-fits-all prescription for creating the change you want in your life. Instead, it reminds you that the journey is deeply personal and that the work of confronting old patterns and behaviors is difficult. But to make a commitment to the work means creating a *Bold New You* that brings you from who you should be to who you were meant to be."

TERESA EYET, VICE PRESIDENT of EDUCATION at AMERICAN HEALTH CARE ASSOCIATION

....

"*Bold New You* brings together all the concepts I've seen Justin apply with executives in our company that have made a difference in how they lead, communicate, and drive results. I am a witness to how these concepts work!"

NICHOLAS BERTRAM, PRESIDENT at GIANT FOOD STORES, LLC

....

"The energy, passion, and enthusiasm that Justin exhibits in person has come to life in his book. He will inspire you and give you the steps and tools to develop the true and authentic leader that you are meant to be."

TERRI STEEB GRONAU, VICE PRESIDENT of DIVISION II at NCAA

....

"Justin has helped grow and inspire over 4,000 Restaurant Managers at Taco Bell. His ability to connect and engage makes him one of the most impactful leaders they interact with while at Taco Bell. He has literally transformed their lives, leaving them better managers and better people. His book, *Bold New You*, now provides all Restaurant Managers in the industry with a guide on how to focus on the one thing they can control: the choice on how they lead."

FRANK TUCKER, CHIEF PEOPLE OFFICER at TACO BELL

"In his book, Justin has captured the same insightful, thought-provoking messages that he's shared in his presentations on stages around the world. He provides no-nonsense approaches to help empower you to be a *Bold New You*. Do yourself a favor, put this book on your MUST-READ list."

DAVE KILBY, PRESIDENT at WESTERN ASSOCIATION OF CHAMBER EXECUTIVES

"In his work, Justin Patton teaches people to become better leaders. With his brilliant new book, B*old New You*, he helps all of us become better people, too. His writing engages and inspires, but it's the book's interactive element that sets it apart as much more than standard motivational fare. With well-considered questions and exercises for his readers, Justin guides us into a more complete relationship with ourselves so that we can show up more compassionately and courageously with others—as a good leader, and a good person, too."

SCOTT STABILE, AUTHOR of *BIG LOVE*

"Are you serious about making personal change? You have found the right book. *Bold New You* guides you through discovery and internalization, and then invites you to take intentional action to be a better you. This book also equips leaders with the questions and exercises to inspire, support, and lead others towards achieving their best as well!"

JAMES FRIPP, CHIEF DIVERSITY AND INCLUSION OFFICER at YUM! BRANDS

"*Bold New You* is relatable, honest, and vulnerable in its perspective. It explores a meaningful pathway to becoming the best version of yourself and to living a life with purpose. Justin helps us to unlock our inner truth with positivity."

AIDAN HAY, SVP of OPERATIONS for THE COFFEE BEAN & TEA LEAF

"Justin Patton's insights into championing your own worth to unleash your fullest potential is a revolutionary combination of proven personal coaching exercises, examples of success, and challenging questions to rediscover a bold new you. The deep inner work and rigorous process you will experience will transform your life, your leadership, and your impact on the world. It is a rare gift and sure to be a powerful bestseller."

VICKI HALSEY PhD, VICE PRESIDENT at THE KEN BLANCHARD COMPANIES

....

"Justin is an individual who speaks to the souls of others—helping them develop their skill sets to become leaders in the business world. His book, *Bold New You*, addresses our ability to transform ourselves into leaders on a personal and business level that many would never have visualized. As an Operations Leader in the restaurant industry, I see Justin's book and his teachings as a guide to creating high performance teams at all levels of an organization."

DEBBIE CARVER, OPERATIONS DIRECTOR at PETERSON BURGE ENTERPRISES

....

"*Bold New You* is one of the most relevant leadership books I've read in years. It is thought-provoking, timeless, and packed full of "aha!" moments. Justin's storytelling, experience as an executive coach, and practical exercises makes this book a must-read for all chamber of commerce leaders and members."

MEGAN LUCAS, CEO at LYNCHBURG REGIONAL BUSINESS ALLIANCE

....

"Justin remains one of our all-time favorite keynote speakers. Our audience of nearly 1,000 unanimously found his content vital to their leadership journey and the delivery of his message to be authentic, engaging, and relatable. Justin's book has been highly anticipated, and it does not disappoint. The passion, raw honesty, and thought-provoking questions led me to new discoveries and realizations that no leader has brought out in me previously."

STACEY BONINE, CORPORATE SERVICES DIRECTOR at ENERGETIC WOMEN, A PROGRAM OF MEA ENERGY ASSOCIATION

"Want to be bold instead of brazen, confident instead of arrogant, assertive instead of aggressive? If so, you will find no better guide in becoming this than this bold and wonderful book. Read it, learn it, practice it and live it, because when you do you will gain the notice and respect of everyone... including yourself."

MARK GOULSTON, M.D., AUTHOR of *JUST LISTEN*

"Reading *Bold New You* is like having this dynamic personal coach right in front of you. *Bold New You* will help you come face to face with yourself—a great first step for new leaders and a perfect reminder for those who have lost their way."

KEITH COLE, PAST PRESIDENT of KFC NORTHEAST FRANCHISE ASSOCIATION

"This book is a must-read for those who are in leadership roles or strive to be. Justin delivers timely, concise, and inspiring advice as he walks you through steps to rediscovering your authentic self. Working in the Chamber industry, I watch how many believe in taking care of others first. *Bold New You* shows how taking care of yourself while still being in a "people-first" mindset works to your advantage and those around you. This book will be in our association library for all the Kentucky chamber professionals to read. Thank you, Justin, for putting your words of wisdom into print."

AMY CLOUD, EXECUTIVE DIRECTOR at KENTUCKY CHAMBER OF COMMERCE EXECUTIVES

"If you're serious about building a world-class organization, then you need to read *Bold New You* by Justin Patton right now. It's insightful, forward-thinking, and immediately actionable, and Justin gives you the road map to become the leader of the future—one who treats people, profit, and purpose as one so you can unlock the "X-factor" of results, revenue, and marketplace success. Buy a copy for everyone. And watch how your team starts to perform at its highest, boldest, and best."

DAVID NEWMAN, AUTHOR of *DO IT! MARKETING*

BOLD NEW YOU
by Justin Patton

Printed in the United States of America.
FIRST EDITION. January 2019.

Bold New You
6 Breakthroughs to Playing Bigger in Leadership, Business, and Life

ISBN 978-1-7328766-5-1 (paperback)
978-1-7328766-0-6 (ebook)

Written by Justin Patton
Cover design and layout by Shaina Nielson
Edited by Chantel Hamilton

DEDICATION

To the unsung heroes in my life:

Mom
Thank you for showing me the power of unconditional love and how you are never too old to learn.

Dad
Thank you for teaching me the meaning of hard work.

Susan
Thank you for always making me laugh and for keeping me grounded.

Victoria and BreeAnna
Thank you for teaching me how to love bigger.

BOLD *new you*

6 Breakthroughs to Playing Bigger in **Leadership**, **Business**, and **Life**

BOLD NEW YOU

ARE YOU READY?

There is no mistake
Where you are in your journey:
You Are Unfinished . . .

September 19, 1998. That was the day my life spiraled out of control and everything changed. I was 18 years old and I had come home from college for the weekend to see my parents. My dad had recently undergone surgery and was recovering, so he was not able to get around much. That morning, however, he took me to get my hair cut and he bought groceries for my college dorm room. Mom had lunch ready for us when we got home, so we all sat at the kitchen table. It was there I knew something was wrong. My dad, at some point in the middle of eating, put down his fork, tilted his head, and started crying. It was the first time I had ever seen my dad cry. He was 46 years old, had served in the Air Force and Vietnam, was a Supervisor of Maintenance Operations at the United States Postal Service, and had a knack for fixing any equipment on our farm. I thought he was unbreakable. I finished lunch and went into the living room where I could eavesdrop on my parents. They were on the phone with the doctor who told my dad to come in the next day so they could check him out, make sure he was okay, and go from there.

That evening my dad was lying in bed with my mom, who was rubbing his chest because it was hurting. He experienced a sharp pain that didn't feel right, so he looked at my mom and said, "If that happens again, I think we should go to the hospital or call the doctor." It happened again, and my dad's eyes rolled back in his head, he gasped one last time, and he died in my mom's arms. The autopsy report indicated that my dad had contracted a bacterial infection that got into his blood stream and shut down his heart.

As an 18-year-old kid who did not know how to cope or deal with a loss that painful and excruciating, I did the only thing I knew how to do which was to emotionally disconnect. Therefore, I emotionally disconnected from everyone in life—including myself. I, subconsciously, dragged the emotional residue and pain of my father's death around with me everywhere I went for over a decade. That choice directly impacted the way I led teams, the way I developed relationships with others, and my ability to authentically connect with people.

I disconnected by suiting up in emotional armor that no one could penetrate. My rationale, at the time, was if I could control protecting myself, and avoid feeling the feelings I didn't want to feel or didn't know how to deal with, then I would never be too hurt or too disappointed. The armor I wore every day felt lighter to me than the weight of my own emotions, so I learned to never take it off.

ARE YOU READY?

All relationships in my life—personal and professional—suffered from my inability to be emotionally available. One of my earliest memories of when I sacrificed a relationship, and my leadership impact, happened in college. I did not agree with a decision made so I went above the person in charge. I ended up getting what I wanted in the end, but I sacrificed my relationship with her, my personal credibility, and any level of trust I had. I was more concerned with being right than learning to take people with me and get results through them.

I desperately wanted to connect with others on a deep level, but I couldn't because I wasn't even connected to myself. As a result, I used my job to validate my self-worth. I sacrificed time with the people who mattered the most to me for a job where people rewarded my ego and let me get away with bad behavior. I achieved great results, but eroded relationships in the process. I wasn't effective at sharing and discussing emotions, so my communication was often cold and detached. I was unaware of the impact my body language and tone had on others. I was overly direct and would justify my actions by saying, "I just tell people how it is." I wore the title of "Truth-Teller" as a badge of honor when it really should have said, "Jerk." More dangerously, I could not have empathy with partners, colleagues, or team members because I did not have empathy for myself. My inability to tune into my emotions and take off the armor prevented me from being open to feedback I needed to hear, from being a leader and coach that inspired engagement and forward movement, and from cultivating relationships built on trust instead of transactions.

My 20-year journey of self-discovery has taught me that you can change your life the moment you are willing to come face to face with yourself. To look at yourself in the mirror and tell the truth about how you are showing up and possibly holding yourself back is one of the scariest and bravest things you will ever do for yourself and others. I realized, around 30 years old, that my actions were self-sabotaging and kept me playing smaller than my potential. I knew I could play bigger and lead better, but I had lost sight of how. I knew if I was going to achieve the type of relationships, success, and life I wanted then I was going to have to look at myself and my life differently.

> You can change your life the moment you are willing to come face to face with yourself.

It is easy to blame our circumstances on others because accountability can be messy, soul-searching work that we are not always ready to do. It is not easy to admit that we gave our power away by letting others treat us less than we deserved, that we talked a big game but didn't always do the work to reach the goals we say we wanted, that we weren't always there for family, employees, and colleagues the way we should have been, or that we got so caught up in being "successful" that we consistently betrayed ourselves in the process. Millions of people spend their entire life without ever living up to their potential. You do not have to be one of them.

I know many of you reading this introduction believe you can play bigger in both your personal and professional life, and I, too, believe you are capable of that. Maybe you want to show up with more confidence, but don't know what you need to do. Maybe you are getting great results, but you are sacrificing relationships with others or the relationship with yourself in the process. Maybe you have been knocked down so hard you do not know how to find your way out anymore. Well, this is your starting point. I am not writing this book because I have all the answers or because I have it all together. In fact, I have made many mistakes. I will share a lot of them as we dive into this process together in hopes that you will be able to see yourself in those stories and realize you are not alone.

BECOMING A BETTER LEADER OF YOURSELF

I landed in Orange County, California and I was making my way to the Taco Bell Restaurant Support Center in Irvine, CA when the Uber driver turned down the music and asked me what I did for a living. I told him that I taught leadership and communication skills. He emphatically stated, "I'm not a leader!" and asked me for programs he could attend.

I believe everyone is a leader, so I was curious as to why he would say this. I asked him, "How are you defining the word 'leader'?" He gave me some long, verbose definition that almost no one would ever live up to. No wonder he didn't think he was a leader! He had defined himself out of his own worthiness. We talked about leadership for a while and how it is about the ability to create influence. We all create influence regardless of our age, sex, race, and income. We influence friends, family, social media followers, people at work, and strangers. It is what we decide to do with the influence we have that ultimately determines how others perceive us. As I was getting out of the car, he turned to me and said, "You know what? I do have influence. I influence my family. I influence my friends. I influence people who get in my car. *I am a leader!*"

I wanted to write a book that empowers individuals, just like you and that Uber driver, to create a radical transformation on how they view themselves so they can be better leaders—for themselves, their families, their communities, and their company. Millions of people get up every morning and look in the mirror at a person they no longer recognize. They do not feel successful because they are not where they believe they should be on their journey. They condemn themselves for their past choices and rather than sit in the messiness of their life and do their work to heal, they protect themselves by emotionally disconnecting and making excuses for their behavior. As a result, they look in the mirror less and less. When we stop looking at the truth of our own reflection, we don't hold ourselves accountable to our own greatness and we act in ways that are incongruent to our best self. More dangerously, we replace action with excuses.

As an international speaker and certified executive coach, I have the privilege of speaking to thousands of leaders every year—from teenagers all the way up to CEOs. My journey has allowed me to work with leaders across the United States and in Russia and Canada. I had the honor of becoming a faculty member for the US Chamber of Commerce and co-facilitated the largest leadership development program in Taco Bell's franchise history. Additionally, I have coached executives in Fortune 500 organizations, NCAA athletes, and contestants in the Miss America and Miss USA pageants. My personal and professional experience has taught and reinforced one fundamental lesson on leadership and success: you cannot be a great leader of others until you first become a great leader of yourself.

> You cannot be a great leader of others until you first become a great leader of yourself.

Everyone benefits when you take the time to become a better leader of yourself, which is the catalyst for why I wrote *Bold New You*. Being bold is defined as demonstrating both confidence and courage, and I intend to help you cultivate more of that by the time you finish this book. It is risky to look at yourself when you are not certain what you will see or what choices you will be asked to make. There is nothing easy about living a bold life. But maybe, just maybe, it is in our boldness that we discover our full potential.

> It is in our boldness that we discover our full potential.

Being bold is not worrying about how other people see you, but about being at peace with the person staring back at you in the mirror. Some people are not going to like the bold new version of you when you start to stand up for yourself, honor your boundaries, express your feelings in a transparent and tactful way, and spend your time on the things that add value to your life. They don't have to like it. They can fall away so better people and opportunities can rise up in their place. History has been shaped by bold leaders—some known and many unknown—who used their boldness to make a bigger mark on this world. You always have the option of being one of them.

I was brought in to work with a Vice President of Finance who was not meeting expectations and who did not show up credible in meetings with peers. The Chief Executive Officer (CEO) believed in this leader and gave me six months to help ignite what he believed was already there. The VP of Finance and I spent the first month of coaching looking in the mirror. I had her back as she sat in some uncomfortable spaces and became more aware and accountable for her part in the current dysfunction. One profound moment of self-awareness was when we discussed that, "You don't have to be the smartest person in the room. You need to be the most strategic and demonstrate exceptional leadership." She spent the next five months speaking up more, living her authentic leadership brand, establishing new boundaries, and accepting that decisions do not impact her identity and self-worth. After five months, the CEO said to her in a one-on-one meeting, "You have been the success story of the year." The Vice President changed both her results and how others perceived her because she had the boldness to be real with herself and others. She proved that a lack of self-awareness is what gets us in trouble. Emotional intelligence is the antidote that pulls you out and up to a bold new version of yourself. Your competence will play a role in helping you get a job, but it is your emotional intelligence that will help you keep it. Being a great leader of yourself requires you to level up on your awareness of yourself, so this book is going to help you do just that!

HOW THIS BOOK IS DIFFERENT

Many of the leadership and communication books I've read provide great content and best practices; however, they do not provide the necessary exercises and empowering questions to help you learn and apply what was shared. They might offer quick fixes to a symptom, but they do not address the core internal issues that prevent leaders from leading and communicating their best. For example, I can teach someone how to have better body language, but if their mindset is still judgmental and critical then their actions are not authentic, the other person will see through it, and trust will still be eroded. More importantly, they end up reverting to the same behavior that was holding them back originally. I am sure you have witnessed this in yourself or others. I am not just going to tell you why purpose, energy, and owning your voice is important in your life. I am going to provide you with tangible exercises, so you discover your purpose, learn how to shift your energy, and use your voice to connect in meaningful ways.

This book is designed to be highly interactive, so there will be individual exercises and discussion questions for you to complete throughout—if you are ready for that step. If you are reading this book with a partner, friend, or as a leadership team then I encourage you to engage in a conversation about your key takeaways. For those of you who believe in the power of mindfulness, I have included an affirmation at the end of every chapter to help you set a positive intention for your day or week as you apply what you learn. Additionally, I have included free downloads, exercises, and video content that you can access on my website at **boldnewyou.com.**

HOW TO READ THIS BOOK

This book is meant to be a road map on how to discover a bold new version of yourself. It would be presumptuous of me or anyone else to believe we know the exact right path for every person to take. There is no one correct way to get you where you want to be, but there are best practices to help you navigate with your eyes wide open and your feet aligned in the direction of your possibilities.

I encourage you to read this book in a way that is meaningful and adds the most value to you. Therefore, you do not have to read the chapters in the order they are presented. My recommendation is that you read the chapters in the order that most aligns with your current needs.

Rank the following statements, on a scale of 1 to 6, in order of importance, with 1 being the most important factor and your biggest opportunity, and 6 being the least important because you are already doing it well. Each statement should have a different number next to it.

- [ ] I want to let go of my past and the negative thoughts that keep me playing small.
- [ ] I want to understand how to keep my ego in check, so it does not erode my relationships and influence.
- [ ] I want to own a mindset and presence that will put me in the place of most potential.
- [ ] I want to learn strategies on how I can own my voice and speak with stronger impact.
- [ ] I want to work on my leadership credibility so I can be a champion for myself and others.
- [ ] I want to live a meaningful life and discover my purpose.

The statements above reflect the order of the six chapters in this book; however, read the chapters in the order that you scored them. I believe it is in that space you can earn some quick wins which will empower you to continue doing this work since you will see the value. Please note: the last three chapters you ranked are just as important as the top three chapters. Do not allow yourself to be any less intentional about reading and applying those concepts to your daily life. It is the purposeful integration of all six chapters that will allow you to play bigger and lead better.

ARE YOU READY?

It has taken me years to put this book together in a way I thought would add value to you. I hope it inspires you; however, this is not meant to be another motivational book that is just going to make you feel good about yourself. Motivation without action is nothing more than good intentions, and you do not transform your life with good intentions. This book is a wake-up call and a resource for you to discover how to start leading better in your life and in the lives of others. It is going to challenge you to own a new mindset so you can take intentional action to get from where you are today to where you want to be tomorrow. Additionally, it is going to require you to get uncomfortable and do the inside work so you can live life on your terms. Throughout my life, I've had some wonderful mentors and coaches who believed in me when I sometimes didn't even believe in myself. These coaches told me the truth when I needed to hear it, listened when I needed to feel like I wasn't alone, and they gave me the insight to play bigger in my life. Therefore, I write this book not as an author, trainer, or speaker, but as your personal coach who understands what you're going through, who does not judge you for where you are today, and who believes you have everything you need to live the life you want if you are willing to do the work. I am not here to change you. I want to help you become more of who you are at your best.

> You do not transform your life with good intentions.

It is no accident that you received this book today. If you bought it for yourself then you have already taken the first step to discovering a bold new version of who you are, and I am honored to be a small part of your magnificent journey. If someone else bought this book for you then they see a spark in you that is just waiting to be ignited. Regardless of how and why you received this book, here is the truth I want you to hear right now: you are not designed to play small. You are unfinished and capable of living and leading even better.

Louise Hay, in her international best-selling book, *You Can Heal Your Life,* says, "We are all just doing the best we know how with the understanding, awareness, and knowledge we have at the time." Being unfinished is recognizing that we did our best with what we had, but we are ready to do better. So, take a deep breath right now and give yourself a break! You showed up and communicated the best you knew how in your relationship, your job, and your family. Your best might have disappointed or even hurt people. Others' best might have disappointed or hurt you. Who you are today does not have to dictate who you are tomorrow! You do not have to live in the guilt and shame of your past actions and who you were not able to be in that moment. You are bigger than any one moment, any one relationship, and any past choice that you have made. You have the option to make a different choice. This book is your invitation.

Courageous action will take you further in life than fear ever will.

It takes both confidence and courage to look at yourself in the mirror, but one thing I know for sure is that courageous action will take you further in life than fear ever will. You are the leader you've been searching for in others, so I hope you will give yourself permission to be that leader. You will never be fully ready for what is next in your life, but do it anyway! Just start and trust that you will learn what you need to learn along the way. You are not alone as you begin this important, and perhaps even audacious, process. This book is your road map and it provides you with six bold steps to playing bigger in leadership, business, and your personal life. Integrating it into your life is not about getting to a defined destination. It is about the constant practice of living up to your potential. It is up to you to take bold action to live the life you want!

Finally, I hope you remember that every day you open your eyes you have the power to choose differently, to choose better, and to choose you! You accept the choice you think you deserve. You are free to live a life bigger and bolder than where you are now. It's time for a bold new you. Let's get to work.

I believe in you.

SET YOUR INTENTION FOR READING THIS BOOK

1. What do you want to get out of this book?

2. How would accomplishing your intention positively impact your life?

CHAPTER ONE
LEADERSHIP SUMMARY

- The most important relationship you have is the one with yourself; therefore, you have no greater responsibility than to take care of you, first.

- Everyone suffers around you when you are not able to show up your best.

- We must get over this notion that taking care of ourselves is selfish. It is not selfish; it is necessary.

- How you treat yourself reflects what you believe you are worth.

- Taking care of yourself and becoming a better leader starts with your ability to redefine success, address your patterns of behavior, forgive yourself and others, invite truth-tellers on your journey, and lean into the possibilities for what is next in your life.

1

want to be a great leader of yourself?

TAKE CARE OF YOU, FIRST

Everyone suffers
When you don't take care of you.
Please, love yourself first!

I received a call from a CEO who said, "I'm tired. I need your help." He was, by most people's standards, highly successful. He was leading and growing multiple businesses, financially well-off, and had a supportive family. As he described his journey, I could tell he spent much of his life acquiring external achievements and, when he accomplished them, he was on the hunt for the next one. I finally asked, "What are you really searching for?" He paused for a few seconds and then replied, "Happiness."

This leader, like many of us, lost himself somewhere in the hustle and bustle of "making it." He put his success in external factors that would never be good enough. He was constantly comparing himself and holding himself to unnecessary expectations. Additionally, his constant need to achieve was triggered by his deep desire to prove that he was good enough. He had found himself physically productive for years while being emotionally exhausted and not showing up his best. He knew if he wanted to be the best leader he could be he had to slow down and take care of himself.

> Servant leadership is about having a people-first mindset.

There will be critics reading this book who say that great leaders don't put themselves first; they put others first. They will talk a lot about servant leadership and give you examples of people who consistently put others before themselves. We have the conversation on servant leadership backwards. Servant leadership is about having a people-first mindset. Putting people first means you make and honor intentional choices to help people and organizations reach their highest possible potential. A people-first mindset means you protect the relationships you have with people and you do your best to always create a win-win outcome. Servant leadership does not require you to forfeit yourself in the process. You are part of that equation. The best leaders are artful in their ability to balance the needs of others with the needs of themselves.

The real conversation we should be having on servant leadership—that often goes unspoken—is that servant leadership starts with you. When you have leaders who do not know themselves or who are emotionally bankrupt, one of two things happen:

1. They only focus on results and bully people into achieving them at any cost.

2. They are overly empathetic, avoid necessary conversations, and often don't hold people accountable.

Someone is always on the losing side of the relationship in both situations, but there is a better way. True servant leadership is about leading with both your head and heart. It means you have the knowledge and the compassion to serve yourself as you would serve others. It is about doing the vulnerable work in order to show up authentically and with positive intent so you build stronger levels of trust and influence. Prioritizing yourself, as you would prioritize others, is a fundamental way to serve others at your best.

> Prioritizing yourself, as you would prioritize others, is a fundamental way to serve others at your best.

We must get over this antiquated notion that your personal life is your personal life and your work life is your work life. There might be leaders who believe this philosophy, but the mentality is outdated, and it is going to prevent them from retaining top talent and building a culture of engagement. The best leaders bring their whole selves to work every day and they are the same person in every part of life. We should not bring just fragments of our whole self to work, and organizations that only want pieces of you do not deserve your time and productivity. It is your authenticity that builds trust and influence with others. Therefore, when you do not take care of your whole self or you do not take the time to master and know yourself, you do not show up your best.

Taking care of yourself and doing the inside work to be a better leader is not easy, and it is why so many people avoid doing it. This work requires you to go deep! It is often uncomfortable and very personal, but it is only by going deep that you can break through the bullshit you've been telling yourself for years, get unstuck and out of your own way, and lead at the level of your potential. You cannot download the best version of yourself when you are no longer awake to who that person even is. Taking care of yourself is a process of slowing down, doing the inside work to really know yourself, and giving yourself radical permission to . . .

1. Redefine success
2. Address your patterns of behavior
3. Forgive yourself and others
4. Invite truth-tellers on your journey
5. Lean into the possibilities for what is next

REDEFINE SUCCESS

Success is an inside job!

You can start taking better care of yourself by redefining what success means to you. Former Starbucks CEO Howard Schultz said, "Success is not sustainable if it is defined by how big you become or by growth for growth's sake. Success is very shallow if it doesn't have emotional meaning." This is why success is an inside job!

Success has emotional meaning when it is deeply rooted in purpose, supported by your core values, and connected to something bigger than yourself. Those key ingredients are all a result of your mindset and do not require anything that is outside of your control and choices. Emotional meaning does not rely on external factors like money, titles, accolades, approval, or trophies. Those elements can be indicators of your hard work and forward momentum, but they do not make you more or less worthy.

Dee was a soccer captain at a Division 1 college. She spent most of her childhood playing soccer because it was the one place she felt like she fit in. She grew up with the notion that her success and self-worth were tied to being an athlete. However, during the second game of her senior year, she was forced to reevaluate who she was and what success meant to her. With just under two minutes left in the first half, her legs got tangled with another player's. Dee heard her knee pop out of place and she fell. Dee was carried off the field only to find out she had torn her anterior cruciate ligament (ACL). The recovery process would take her over nine months following surgery. This experience forced Dee to redefine how she would lead her team and be successful. She admitted it was difficult because being on the field is where she believed she added value. She was not sure how to do it from the sidelines. She told me the injury forced her to step back and to see life and leadership from a different perspective. Ironically, because Dee was more available and present for others, she earned more trust from her teammates and people came to her more for advice. She said, "In the beginning, I felt like I was a disappointment to people. I couldn't fulfill their expectations on the field. However, I've realized life is so much more than soccer. Soccer has brought me joy. It has taught me valuable lessons, but it is not who I am."

Dee's story reminds all leaders that you set yourself up for perpetual disappointment when you define your success by external factors for two core reasons. Firstly, you allow your success to be determined by the randomness of life and the opinion of others because you anchor your happiness and sense of worth to those outcomes. Secondly, external factors are not a realistic and sustainable way to measure your success because you are always on the hunt for something bigger and better. The problem is the luster of these accomplishments wears off and we discover that the external fix wasn't enough. We find ourselves unhappy again, so we start over on our quest for something deeper and more fulfilling.

That was my life during my twenties. I was addicted to the praise and recognition of my actions. My intent behind working so hard was so others would tell me how much they appreciated me. It was a drug that only provided a short-term fix. When it wore off, I was on a hunt for the next one. I had a boss sit me down one day and say, "Justin, I want you to think about this. When you are working late every day, on the weekends, on holidays, and not spending time with the people you say you love the most, I want you to stop and ask, 'What are you avoiding?'" The truth is, I was avoiding myself. I wasn't comfortable with the person in the mirror, so I didn't spend much time looking there. As a result, I was overwhelmed, overworked, and overcommitted. I had done it all to myself and other people suffered as a result.

Redefining success and creating emotional meaning in my life started when I took the time to understand my core values. I couldn't possibly bring my whole self to work when I did not know who that person was or what was important to me. One of my first mentors said to me, "If you value it, you'll make time for it." Understanding my core values allowed me to be more intentional about how I led and how I prioritized what I made time for.

Many people believe it is external factors—home, job, or other people—that make them fulfilled and successful. However, when they describe their values and what they stand for (i.e., family, spirituality, impact, security) you realize they feel successful because their external factors align back to who they say they are. It is their values that are driving their success. That's the inside work in action!

CONNECTING SUCCESS TO YOUR CORE VALUES

1. List the three factors that currently make you feel successful in your life (i.e., family, job, home).

2. Identify your top four core values. To download and complete a core values exercise go to boldnewyou.com.

3. Summarize how your three factors align with your core values and who you say you are.

4. How does this challenge you to look at success differently?

ADDRESS YOUR PATTERNS OF BEHAVIOR

A colleague and I were delivering a leadership and communications program early on in my career. During her portion of the program, I found myself interjecting and adding what I considered illuminating commentary for the audience. Afterwards, I could tell she was upset. She felt my repeated "profound insight" undermined her credibility, and I remember her storming off to her car. I attempted to justify my behavior with some lame excuse I believed was rational at the time. However, looking back, she was right. Being emotionally detached for a long period of my life impacted my leadership credibility and my ability to develop meaningful relationships that served both people. I often failed to understand the impact my actions had on others, and I am embarrassed to admit that sometimes I did not even care. This pattern of behavior, that I demonstrated in every aspect of my life, kept me playing smaller than my potential.

When I was unaware of how I used detachment to protect myself emotionally, I would bail out of relationships at the first sign of a problem. I could never fully trust others or allow people to have my back at work or at home. I always had one hand ready to catch myself because then I wouldn't have to worry about others disappointing me or not meeting my expectations. All my relationships lacked intimacy and vulnerability, thus making it harder to authentically connect. I was a driver in business meetings and relentless in achieving goals. However, in the process of achieving those goals I often failed to take people with me. Only when I became aware that I emotionally detach from both personal and professional relationships could I start to make some conscious choices to experience life differently and start playing bigger.

I coached a military veteran who served in the armed forces for over 20 years. He explained that in the service many leaders have a "move up or move out" mentality. With changing jobs every couple of years, you only have about 12 months to prove yourself before being considered for your next promotion. This means you have to hit the ground running and quickly make your mark in order to advance to the next level. This philosophy aligned with his driving personality and his ability to create exceptional results. However, after leaving the military and returning to civilian life, he found himself dissatisfied and unsettled after being in non-military jobs for a period of time. The military had provided structure and clarity when it came to each level of advancement, so he felt lost and always searching for more without this. During one of our conversations he was considering another career change. This time, however, he realized that maybe it wasn't his intuition telling him to make a career decision, but the pattern of behavior he acquired while in the military. He was able to make a more informed choice when he understood how this behavior was impacting his internal monologue and decision-making process.

Our patterns of behavior are dangerous when we do not realize we are dragging them around everywhere we go. This is why self-awareness is one of the most important elements for leaders to cultivate. Our internal baggage always shows up in our external behavior. When we tune into these patterns, and stop believing other people are the ones creating all the problems in our lives, we become more emotionally intelligent and better leaders of ourselves.

IDENTIFY YOUR PATTERNS OF BEHAVIOR

1. What patterns of behavior that hold you back do you find yourself demonstrating, based on what you've been through in your life?

2. If you are struggling to answer, consider these questions:

    a. What constant "issues" do you find yourself experiencing with others?

    b. What behaviors prevent you from connecting?

    c. What unwanted relationships or situations do you repeatedly find yourself in?

d. What feedback do you consistently receive from others?

e. Do you say, "People always treat me this way?" What is "this way"?

3. What impact are your patterns having on your relationships, your joy, your success, and your peace?

4. How are you now contributing to the ongoing cycle of this pattern in your life?

5. What is one specific step you can implement this week to break the cycle?

"I let people 'all in' and then I live in fear of them leaving me." This vulnerable admission was from a leader I had the opportunity to coach in 2017. She, like many of us, walked around with an unreconciled fear-story that shaped how she showed up in every relationship in her life. These fear-stories often form our patterns of behavior. We create these deep-rooted narratives to protect ourselves, but they fester and materialize into an unhealthy and untrue script that we repeat over and over, to the point where they no longer serve us. As she sat, quietly, on the other end of the phone, I asked her, "What actions do you demonstrate when you are so afraid of that individual leaving you?" She replied, "I try to control the situation. I put up with stuff I shouldn't because I don't say anything. I over-analyze all the time, and I get caught up trying to prove how lovable I am."

Her destructive patterns of behavior were rooted in a fear-story, as is the case for most of us. That fear-story is always, "I am not good enough." I have found, however, that under the word "good" is usually something much deeper that gets to the core of what is unreconciled in your life. Examples I have seen with clients I have coached: "I'm not lovable enough", "I'm not smart enough", "I'm not attractive enough", "I'm not normal enough", and "I'm not fun enough." Our fear-story might sound irrational when we say it out loud, but we have subconsciously believed the narrative because of what we have experienced. Our fear-story is always looking for opportunities to prove its reality. Therefore, if you give it a starring role in your life, it will win an Oscar for Best Performance! When we don't know how to rewrite a narrative for our life then we cling to the old one—even if it's no longer serving us. Your relationships, personally or professionally, cannot survive people's unresolved fear-stories. The antidote is awareness.

Your fear-story shoots you full of raw emotion and it becomes lethal to your self-esteem. It turns you into a best-selling author who creates a lot of great stories about other people's behavior—but these are never rooted in facts, just fear. When you are unaware of why you feel what you feel, you will spend a lot of energy proving the fear-story wrong. Consequently, your actions often manifest as the very thing you tried so hard to prevent.

I coached a senior executive whose fear-story was, "I'm not smart enough." This story was birthed from a boss who belittled her, questioned her competence, and never showed her any appreciation. For years, she would drag this fear-story behind her to board meetings and into difficult conversations with peers. When she felt challenged, she sensed the need to prove how smart she was. Her behavior, as a result, came across as desperate and inauthentic. Sometimes it made her get flustered, other times overly assertive, and it often caused her to just retreat and be silent. All those actions eroded her credibility and the perception others had of her.

Your fear-story will always challenge you to live up to its expectations. That story of you not being good enough might feel true in the moment you've been dealt bad news, or someone doesn't respond the way you want them to, or when things do not go as planned. However, just because something might feel true in the moment does not mean it is the truth of who you are at your core.

Your lack of awareness of the patterns of behavior you drag around every day leaves you subconsciously biased to the life you've always had. You can do better. We take better care of ourselves and our relationships when we learn to address our fear-story and uncover the patterns of behavior we demonstrate when we believe in its madness. We cannot expect leaders to be authentic or lead from an inclusive space until they've done the inside work to transform their fear-story. In Harold S. Kushner's best-selling book, *When Bad Things Happen to Good People*, he writes, "Pain makes some people bitter and envious. It makes others sensitive and compassionate. It is the result, not the cause, of pain that makes some experiences of pain meaningful and others empty and destructive." Being a great leader of yourself requires you to make something meaningful come from all your experiences.

MY FEAR–STORY IS

Every fear-story is rooted in the belief that "I'm not good enough." Under the word "good" is something much deeper based on what you have experienced. What is your fear-story?

1. Identify your fear-story: I am not _____ enough!

2. Recall the first time you had that thought.

3. What purpose did you give that thought when you first created it?

4. Identify examples in your life of how that story has been reinforced.

5. How has that thought impacted your actions?

6. How is this fear-story preventing you from showing up as the type of person you want to be?

7. Who would you be without that thought?

CAUTION: *do not become so caught up in "fixing" your fear-story that you fail to transform it.* Sometimes we become so accustomed to fixing immediate needs that we fail to address, learn, and transform the core of what is holding us back.

I have spent the majority of my life self-conscious and obsessed with my weight. I complain and talk about it a lot. Hell, it is exhausting for me—so I know it is exhausting for everyone around me. The most logical thing would be for me to implement some quick fixes by participating in workout classes, eliminating certain foods, and doing meal preparation. This is not a bad place to start. It is imperative, however, if we are going to be great leaders of ourselves that this is not where the work ends. Over time, I learned the core of my problem was never about my weight. The weight was just the symptom of a much deeper fear. The issue was the meaning I attached to my weight. I remember being at home one day and asking myself, "So, what does it mean if you are fat?" My vulnerable response was, "Then I won't be lovable enough and I will find myself alone." I had attached my weight to my lovability, and I had starved myself out of the self-love I deserved. As a result, I had emotionally disconnected and therefore didn't know how to show authentic intimacy. I thrived on people's compliments about my looks, I found satisfaction in how many likes I received on social media, and when I did receive validation I deflected it or refused to believe it. Professionally, I became relentless in my career because I was on a mission to prove that I could be good enough in other areas of my life, I become addicted to the next accolade or big "opportunity" as managers would frame it, and, as a result, I lacked any semblance of balance. It was only with my awareness of this deep-rooted fear that I could start to make some different choices. Had I focused solely on the immediate, short-term fixes, I never would have been able to transform and heal myself at the level I needed to if I was going to show up my best. More importantly, the results would not have been sustainable in the long term.

Someone once gave me the sage advice to "sit in the bathwater." So often when the bathwater gets cold or the film starts to form on the top we want to jump up, get out, or add something else to it so we don't have to sit in discomfort. It is often in this discomfort that we can see ourselves, say the things we normally wouldn't say, and learn much deeper lessons about ourselves. So, get out your candles, drop in your favorite bath bombs, and sit in the bathwater until you learn what you need to learn. Some of the best learning opportunities in your life will never be a quick fix or a straight line from point A to B. Remember: the path to transformation starts with awareness but it is a long and windy road. Trust the curves.

Have you ever been around that person who was more addicted to the drama of telling their story than learning from it and moving forward with their life? Emotional healing requires you to acknowledge your past without indulging it. Emotional indulgence keeps you a victim. This happens when you become more addicted to telling the story of what happened than you are to the choices that could help you heal and move on. You indulge in your victimhood because of the comfort it brings you in the moment. You tell your story and others jump feet first into the mess with you, want to know all the salacious details, and make you feel like the star of your own reality television show. The intoxicating validation of the limelight keeps you focused on being more of a storyteller than a healer. Acknowledgment is honoring that the experience happened, recognizing that you have the right to feel whatever you are feeling, creating clarity on what the experience taught you, and then taking intentional action based on what you learned.

Finally, clarity is at the core of your emotional healing. The problem is that when we go through something traumatic we rely on others to give us the clarity we seek. We want God to reveal why He took someone from us. We want our partner to explain why they really left. We want our boss to explain why they made that decision. I have spent countless days stuck in my pain waiting for someone else to give me the clarity I wanted. I have come to realize that, most often, no one else is going to offer you this. More importantly, you do not have the time to wait around seeking an answer that will never fulfill your painful curiosity. It is up to you to provide yourself with the insight you need. The best leaders focus on the things in their control, and creating clarity in your life is at the heart of owning your personal power. It is our ability to generate meaning from pain that gives us the necessary foundation to forgive, move forward, and be better leaders—for ourselves and for others.

CLARITY EXERCISE: FROM PAIN TO MEANING
The following exercise is intended to help you stay connected to both your head- and heart-space and to help you shift from victimhood to seeing the opportunity. This exercise should be done over a period of time while you're struggling to make sense of an experience. Enter the five categories into the notes section of your cell phone or a notebook. Record your thoughts, feelings, or ideas in the appropriate category as they come up. Do this for as long as you need until you feel you have acknowledged what you're feeling and created the clarity you need for yourself.

- I feel . . .
- I am proud of . . .
- I need to own and/or recognize . . .
- I need to forgive . . .
- I learned . . .

FORGIVE YOURSELF AND OTHERS

I had a falling out with my boss, someone I considered a good friend and mentor, in 2012. She and I had a very different perspective on the direction of my career and development. As a result, I made the difficult choice to leave the organization. For over a year, I was bitter about how the relationship and job ended. I spent that year telling as many people as I could about her actions and the drama of how my career at this organization unfolded. The more I told the story, the more people validated my feelings. My unresolved emotions about what happened kept me addicted to telling the story and unable to move forward in a healthy way. Eventually, I was having lunch in Los Angeles with Dr. Mark Goulston, author of *Just Listen*. I told him the story, he looked at me and kindly said, "Why don't you forgive her?" I am sure I choked on my food and then, in a dramatic fashion, I assertively said, "Hell no!"

It took me six months from that conversation to realize Dr. Goulston was right. I became aware that any time a relationship fails, both people have a part to play and I needed to own my part in the relationship. Therefore, I sent her an email and asked if we could talk so I could apologize. We got on the phone a week later and I told her I was sorry for how our relationship ended,

I was grateful for all she had done for me, and I wished things had ended differently. She appreciated my comments and then said, "You don't have to apologize, Justin. I would have done a lot of things differently in hindsight."

This experience taught me that forgiveness is a fundamental step in taking care of ourselves. It invites us to slow down, do the gritty work to heal, and experience what it is like to navigate through life undistracted by all we see in the rear-view mirror. When we offer forgiveness to ourselves or others we make a conscious choice to experience life differently, to walk taller and lighter in our truth, and to write a different ending to our story. Forgiveness shifts us out of a victim mentality and empowers us to be a better leader of ourselves.

We often do not even realize all the choices available to us when we are addicted to the drama and pain of our experiences. Attachment to those experiences is what keeps us emotionally stuck and disconnected. It is at the core of what makes forgiveness difficult. We become so attached to the story of what happened or how we think something should be that the pain consumes us. We hold onto this pain, which often manifests as anger and sadness, because we can control it. It does not require vulnerability or any type of self-reflection on how we contributed to the chaos of the situation. Our anger allows us to be both victim and jury, and our ego loves that space! More dangerously, we subconsciously carry that drama and pain into every conversation and every interaction in our life. This lack of awareness shapes our intentions, our emotional triggers, and the energy we show up with every day. Dr. Goulston helped me see how forgiveness is at the core of our ability to heal, move forward, and not take resentment and lack of trust into other relationships. Making the decision to connect with my former boss was a choice I needed for my emotional healing, not hers. It was me choosing to rise up out of my victimhood, put myself first, and to say what I needed to say so I could move forward.

How we define forgiveness impacts whether or not we believe it is possible. Many people have written about forgiveness, but the definition Oprah Winfrey learned from one of the guests on her show is the one that resonates with me the most. He said, "Forgiveness is giving up the hope that the past could be any different." Giving up hope on the past starts with surrendering the internal "what if" war. What if I had done this? What if we had done that? When you truly accept that you, or the other person, have done the best you could with the awareness and baggage you were dragging around you are able to believe that it could not have been any different. This does not mean you don't hurt and feel the painful reality of the experience. It means you allow the depth of your pain to be met by the depth of your compassion.

At the beginning of this chapter I told you about a CEO who was searching for happiness. He saw his ability to take care of everyone in his company and in his personal life as an honorable thing to do. As a result, he consistently prioritized everyone else's needs above his own. He even felt guilty for talking with me and taking time to invest in himself. I asked him during our conversation, "What do you need to forgive yourself for?" His singular answer created a seismic shift in his perspective and in his willingness to let go of his guilt so he could lean into the bold new version of himself. Forgiveness opens the door to a world full of other possibilities. Forgiveness is just as important in business as it is in our personal life because a lack of forgiveness can bring a whole host of emotions with it that we carry with us everywhere: anger, sadness, resentment, guilt, and skepticism. We instantly become better leaders of ourselves, and others, when we make a choice to be heart-full versus hurt-full.

Lewis B. Smedes, author of *The Art of Forgiving*, says, "Forgiving does not erase the bitter past. A healed memory is not a deleted memory. Instead, forgiving what we cannot forget creates a new way to remember. We change the memory of our past into a hope for our future." Leaders who practice forgiveness, who can let things go that do not serve their best self, and who do not hold themselves or others hostage to perceived mistakes will fundamentally be the best leaders who inspire connection and trust. The bridge between your suffering and your healing is forgiveness.

AN ACT OF FORGIVENESS
Who and what do you need to forgive so you can move forward in your life?

INVITE TRUTH–TELLERS ON YOUR JOURNEY

Truth-tellers are that core group of people you trust to have your back, who love you enough to tell you the truth, and who don't allow you to excuse yourself out of greatness. Our growth requires us to have truth-tellers in our lives.

One of my truth-tellers during the course of writing *Bold New You* was Scott Stabile. Scott is the author of the book *Big Love*—which challenges everything you thought you knew about love, forgiveness, and how to move forward in life. There were several times while writing that I found myself frustrated, questioning what I was doing, and wondering if I was good enough to write this book. I needed to talk with someone who had been there, understood everything I was feeling, and could help me get out of my own way. Scott did that. As my truth-teller, he was there when I needed him. He listened with a wide-open heart, he offered advice when I asked him for it, he wasn't afraid to challenge me when I was speaking nonsense, and he championed me to keep going. His demonstration of love and truth challenged me to play bigger— and that's what all truth-tellers should do.

> It is in the vulnerable space of a tribe you trust that you will exponentially accelerate your awareness and growth.

We must get over the notion that we need to do our inside work and emotional healing all alone. It is irresponsible and unreasonable. It can feel natural to want to retreat and do our work on our own when we go through a difficult time or when we are cultivating specific goals, but our progress is much slower and more painful. It is in the vulnerable space of a tribe you trust that you will exponentially accelerate your awareness and growth.

If you have ever participated in a leadership development program where you were with a cohort of people for an extended period, then you understand the power of a tribe. A tribe is made up of truth-tellers, and those truth-tellers become champions in your life. These individuals make you feel less alone. Their presence ignites trust and safety. They aren't afraid to open up, and the more they open up the more it gives you permission to do the same. Truth-tellers are the people you trust to give you feedback because you know their intent is coming from a good place. They have your back when you need them—and even when you might feel like you don't. Their actions make you feel valued and important. It becomes much easier to drop your defenses, be vulnerable, and ask for help when you realize how important you are to your truth-tellers.

Brené Brown is a thought leader on shame and vulnerability. I believe her work is a must-read for anyone who wants to be a better leader of themselves. One of the many lessons I learned from her courses is that, "shame only survives in silence." Shame cannot survive inside of us when we have the courage to speak it aloud and share it with others. When we keep our emotions silent, they create an internal monologue that stalks us everywhere we go. When we have the courage to give a voice to our emotions and share it with others we trust, we learn deeper lessons, we process the information in healthier ways, and we eliminate bullshit assumptions we made up about ourselves. Truth-tellers are the people you can share the parts of yourself that you don't want anyone else to know.

Leaning in and sharing your thoughts and emotions with your truth-tellers is not about wallowing in your trauma or reclaiming what you lost. It's about releasing pain and shame, and constructing the life you want moving forward. Your commitment to take care of and heal yourself is your declaration to the world, "I am not my past, so join me right where I am or kindly leave me." However, there will be people in your life who try to hold you to the person you've always been and who even reinforce the patterns of behavior you have been hauling around for a long time. The bold new you does not have time for games and manipulation! As you invite truth-tellers on your journey, remove emotional terrorists who would hold you to your past or stop you from achieving the bold new version of yourself.

Emotional terrorists are dangerous and destructive to relationships because their righteous indignation becomes an ideology which allows them to justify their bad behavior. Instead of co-creating a relationship that works for both people, they abuse others to create a relationship that works solely for themselves. They use the most sensitive and vulnerable things they have learned about you against you. They take the trust you put in them and they turn around and use it as a psychological weapon to whittle you into submission and out of your own self-worth. They confuse their manipulation for anger and then they feel their apologies can somehow patch the internal cracks they've inflected. They. Are. Wrong. This might have worked with the old you, but you are not that person any more.

We become co-conspirators in the terrorism when we stay in these relationships longer than we should because we normalize and rationalize their behavior. Time after time, I see people go back to the same dysfunction of a boss, a lover, or a friend because that is all they know. Do not normalize dysfunction in your life. When you remain in that space long enough you become unable to see the truth of what is really going on around you. The dysfunction you know can feel safer than the freedom you don't, so it is easy to sacrifice yourself for what is familiar. It is denial that holds us back from growth, not other people! You will be tested to stand up for who you are. Don't let yourself down. Your self-worth and happiness sometimes lie on the unfamiliar side. You cannot negotiate with an emotional terrorist. Emotional terrorists are cancerous to your growth. Cut them out, and focus your energy on your truth-tellers.

> It is denial that holds us back from growth, not other people!

IDENTIFY YOUR TRUTH-TELLERS

1. Outline the top three truth-tellers in your personal life.

2. Outline the top three truth-tellers in your organization.

3. Outline the top three truth-tellers in your specific area of expertise.

4. Outline the top three truth-tellers in your customer base.

5. Review your list and identify the relationships where you need to invest more time and energy. What will you specifically do over the next month?

6. Explore the names of individuals you would like to add as truth-tellers in the future. How will you get connected and start investing in those relationships moving forward?

LEAN INTO THE POSSIBILITIES FOR WHAT IS NEXT

Your healing and success are directly connected to your ability to lean into all the possibilities for what is next in your life. This mindset is about choosing to not be defined by the trauma, pain, and impact of your past experiences, but using them as lessons that shape you into the person you aspire to be and let you work towards what you want to achieve. It is our commitment to working towards these possibilities that keeps us motivated and engaged in life. It is our ability to set goals and work towards something meaningful that is directly connected to our overall well-being and happiness. When we move intentionally forward in the direction of our goals, we find possibilities can turn into realities, and, with every small victory, we start to believe more and more in the bold new version of ourselves.

Your lack of vision about who you want to be and what you want to achieve is what often keeps you stuck and unsure about how to move forward. Leaning into the possibilities for what is next in your life starts by answering this empowering question: who is the person I aspire to be?

The answer requires you to step out of who you are today and create a vision for what you want the next bold version of yourself to look like. I have heard leaders say, "I want to stop seeing everyone in life as competition." "I want to be the voice of reason, not the counterargument." "I want to be awake to my value." "I want to learn how not to exhaust people." "I want to be humble in heart but strong in mind." "I want to kick fear's ass." The clarity of your answer will help you make some choices that will help you move forward in your life.

THE PERSON I ASPIRE TO BE

Answer the following questions to help you create a vision and action steps on how to move forward:

1. Who is the person you aspire to be?

2. How has what you have been through, and the lessons you have learned, prepared you to achieve this vision?

3. What actions do you need to stop doing to be more of that version of yourself?

4. What actions do you need to continue or start doing to be more of that version of yourself?

5. What are the personal and professional rewards for working towards this vision?

6. What does success look like?

7. How will you measure success on your journey? Identify small wins that you can celebrate along the way.

Redefining success, addressing your patterns of behavior, and forgiving yourself and others are an invitation for you to go on an emotional, soul-searching journey to discover a bold new you. I cannot promise you it will get better anytime soon, but what will happen—if you apply these concepts in your life—is you will learn to move through life stronger and with more resilience. You will be a better leader of yourself! Don't rush your growth, however. Sit in the discomfort. Feel what you need to feel. Create the clarity you need, but crawl out of your pain the moment you find yourself indulging it. Above all else: lean into all the prospects for what is next in your life. Your possibilities are a result of your choices. You might feel stuck now, but these choices lead to freedom. Second chances are simply an opportunity to make the next right decision.

Working on ourselves is not an easy or comfortable process, but we do it because of the possibilities. The possibilities of a better you, a better relationship, a better career, and a better life. When we don't allow ourselves to fall completely apart, we patch the cracks in our heart and try to clog our emotional holes so we don't have to feel the pain. It doesn't work because we feel like "damaged goods" and we disconnect from ourselves and others in hope of preventing any more cracks or holes. You must be willing to fall completely apart so you have the freedom to put yourself back together in a way that best serves you and who you want to be. Remember: everyone benefits when you slow down long enough to take care of yourself. In these moments of fear and vulnerability, you find the birthplace of growth. Keep going. Keep leaning into what is next. Keep discovering the possibilities. You don't have to get it right every time. You just have to be aware enough to know when you don't get it right, so you can slow down and make it right—for yourself and for your relationships. You are worth that choice.

AFFIRMATION

I acknowledge that taking care of myself is a fundamental choice for me to be a great leader of myself. The better I am at taking care of me, the better I am at showing up for others. So, today I will not put myself last. I will be aware of what I am feeling and find meaningful moments to re-energize when necessary. Re-energizing might come in the form of a walk, meditation, prayer, a long bath, talking to someone I love, forgiving myself or others, or making progress on a goal I've been putting off. When I take care of myself, I will feel lighter, more confident, and I will show up with the energy that reflects my character. That is the person I want to be. That is the person I am. I owe it to myself and others to take care of myself, first.

- Authentic empowerment is your best defense in a world bingeing on likes and unrealistic expectations.

- You become authentically empowered when the inner truth of who you are aligns with the outer image you project to the world.

- Ego is any fear-based thought that pulls you out of alignment with the truth of who you are.

- We all have an ego. It is one's lack of awareness that they have an ego that is the problem.

- The biggest consequence of ego is disconnection.

- Your ego manifests itself in one of two extremes: bravado or self-doubt.

- When you operate from your ego you lose self-awareness, your love comes out backwards, denial becomes your biggest defense, and you ultimately erode your self-confidence.

KEEP YOUR EGO IN CHECK

2

want to be a great leader of yourself?

KEEP YOUR EGO IN CHECK

*Stop trying to be
Seen, special, something, someone.
You already are!*

The way we live our life and show up in the world completely changes the moment we make a conscious choice to start acting like we belong—without the need of approval from others. In fact, a stranger I met on a plane in 2016 taught me how dangerous it is when we live our lives trying to "prove" ourselves to everyone else. Steven, at first, was like most other businessmen I meet on planes. He was a professional guy who was married, had kids, and was just doing his best to provide for the people he loved the most. Halfway through the flight, however, Steven divulged that he was about to begin the process of transitioning into a woman. He was, naturally, scared about the impact this would have on his family, but he acknowledged that he could no longer live his life playing a part. Steven shared that it was only on his travels out of town where he felt safe enough to show up as Lacy. When his trips came to an end, he would pack up her clothes and stuff her back into a suitcase. He said, "It wasn't just the clothes I was putting in there. I was packing up my self-worth and identity as well." The past two years have not been easy for Lacy. Standing in our truth never is. Lacy is in the process of getting divorced, her job was eliminated, her mother passed away from cancer, and she had to renegotiate all the relationships in her life. Through everything, Lacy found herself and is no longer looking for permission or approval from anyone else. She affirmed that she became happier when she acted like she belonged. Today, Lacy is in multiple leadership roles in the transgender community, speaking across the country, and an advocate for people showing up as their authentic selves.

Most of us will never have Lacy's story, but all of us have had times in our lives when we found ourselves trying to live up to other people's expectations, played a part we thought we needed to so we could get where we wanted, or felt like we had to prove to others how smart, fabulous, and lovable we really are. Those actions are always a result of our ego and they do not honor our best self. Lacy's story is a reminder to all of us that when we do not see ourselves, we rely on others to see us for who they want us to be. We will try hard to adhere to their version of us while letting ourselves down. Acting like you belong isn't behaving in a way that you believe others want from you. Acting like you belong is showing up as your authentic and tactful-but-unapologetic self. However, it is hard to show up authentically when you have lost sight of who that person is.

In the *Harvard Business Review* article, "Discovering Your Authentic Leadership," the authors say, "Leadership has many voices. You need to be who you are, not try to emulate somebody else [. . .] The journey to authentic leadership begins with understanding the story of your life." However, when we do not slow down long enough to understand who we are, we create a picture we want the world to see and we do whatever it takes to live up to this image—even if that means we are miserable as a result.

Your best defense in a world binging on likes and unrealistic expectations is authentic empowerment. Authentic empowerment, according to Gary Zukav in his best-selling book, *The Seat of the Soul,* is, "when the personality comes fully to serve the energy of its soul." He goes on to talk about the importance of aligning these two constructs. Zukav's ideas have challenged me to think differently and they have been a driving force behind my growth and development over the years. As a result, I have come to believe that a common definition we can all agree with, regardless of our different opinions, is that authentic empowerment is when the inner truth of who you are aligns with the outer image you project to the world. That is when you find your inner champion. That is when you own your personal power. That is when you are no longer trying to prove to the world how great and talented you are because you know your truth, and you are willing to stand boldly in it. It takes intentionality and awareness to keep your inner truth in alignment with your outer image. Do not be mistaken: your ego will always pull you out of alignment. Your ego is the nemesis to your authenticity, so it is up to you to be aware of what your ego is, how it shows up, and the impact it has on your life. It is with this awareness that you can make some different choices.

WHAT IS EGO?

There are so many different perspectives on what ego is and whether it is necessary and empowering or superfluous and destructive. I would like to offer you my viewpoint that is an amalgamation of everything I've studied and learned after speaking to thousands of people every year.

Ego is any fear-based thought that pulls you out of alignment with the truth of who you are. Your inner truth is what many people refer to as your "higher self." It is not up to me or anyone else to tell you what your truth is. It is imperative that you get a clear vision of who you are when you

> Ego is any fear-based thought that pulls you out of alignment with the truth of who you are.

are at your best. However, you will know you are coming from a place of ego the moment your thoughts and actions no longer agree with your higher self.

HOW TO FIND THE TRUTH OF WHO YOU ARE

1. Recall a specific time when you believe you showed up your best.

2. What actions did you demonstrate in that moment?

3. What did you feel in that moment?

4. Taking into consideration those actions, your life experiences, your values/beliefs, how would you finish this line, "At my best, I am ... "

Examples:
At my best, I am confident, kind, and stand up for myself and others.
At my best, I am a messenger of radical love.
At my best, I am fearless.

That is the truth of who you are! And now your job is to ensure your choices align with that truth.

Greg Creed, CEO of Yum! Brands told me, "If there is no fear with the decisions you make then you're not being courageous at all. Fear is attached to courageous behavior." What you can do, however, is allow yourself to experience fear without letting it pull you out of your authentic self. The moment fear causes you to react in ways that are not congruent with your higher self, you erode your character. It is fear-based thoughts that drive your inner critic, influence your posturing, and thwart your self-awareness. The biggest consequence of ego is that it fosters disconnection. You become detached from the truth of who you are and act in ways that are beneath you. As a result, those actions drive disconnection between you and others. All relationships suffer when you lean into your ego more than you lean into your inner truth.

WHAT EGO LOOKS AND FEELS LIKE

I teach leadership classes for the US Chamber of Commerce and during our talks on authentic leadership I ask participants whether they think people who demonstrate ego have a good amount of self-esteem or lack self-esteem. The leaders resoundingly shout, "They lack self-esteem!"

You erode your sense of self-worth and you eventually forget who you are when you nourish your ego more than your inner truth. How we deal with feelings of inadequacy looks and feels different based on the individual. It is those feelings that shape our posturing and what others ultimately experience from us.

Our ego pulls us out of alignment with the truth of who we are, and it always catapults us to an extreme version of ourselves. When this happens, our mindset and actions show up in one of two ways: bravado or self-doubt. So often we associate ego with only arrogance. In fact, Ryan Holiday in his book, *Ego is the Enemy*, defines ego as, "an unhealthy belief in your own importance." Individuals who respond from a place of bravado mask their fear with aggression and armor and go out to face the world with this over-the-top façade of confidence. However, I believe this is only half of the ways in which people respond. Others respond to their fear by surrendering every ounce of their personal power. Their posturing comes across as self-doubt and instead of living their life as a champion for themselves and others, they become victims. The longer we reside in any extreme space, the more comfortable we get. The more comfortable we get, the more we believe that is our authentic self. Do not be fooled: the best version of you never operates in extreme places.

> The best version of you never operates in extreme places.

Below is a chart that outlines some of the core differences in ego posturing.

	BRAVADO	SELF-DOUBT
ASSUMED ROLE	Hero	Victim
COMMUNICATES THEIR TRUTH	Aggressive— without tact	Reserved— does not share
PERSPECTIVE	Future-focused— only looks ahead	Past-focused— only looks back
TRUST	Only trusts themselves	Doesn't trust anyone
SPACE	Takes up a lot of space	Takes up little space
EYE CONTACT	Intimidation	Avoidance
LISTENING	Focused on fixing and being right	Focused on how this applies to themselves
JUDGMENT	Critical of everyone else	Critical of themselves
ACCOUNTABILITY	Blames everyone else	Takes full responsibility, but does not change behavior

HOW DOES YOUR EGO SHOW UP MOST OFTEN?

1. Review the chart of ego posturing.

2. What actions do you demonstrate when you experience fear and step out of the truth of who you are?

3. How do those actions impact your relationships? Your influence?

FOUR IMPACTS OF EGO ON YOUR LIFE

The impact ego has on your life is ubiquitous. At its core, ego drives disconnection. It is the wedge between you and your authenticity. Ego always disconnects you from yourself and others. You might make it to the top of an organization or achieve high levels of financial success with ego, but you will often find yourself standing there alone, isolated, and cynical. You can be surrounded by copious amounts of people and still be alone when your relationships have no depth and no intimacy. Is that really how you want to define success in your life? Below are four of the biggest impacts ego has on your life and your ability to lead yourself.

EGO IS A MALIGNANCY ON YOUR AWARENESS

The aforementioned *Harvard Business Review* article, "Discovering Your Authentic Leadership," states that, "when the 75 members of the Stanford Graduate School of Business Advisory Council were asked to recommend the most important capability for leaders to develop, their answer was nearly unanimous: self-awareness." Self-awareness is easily defined as the ability to look in the mirror and tell the truth about who you are and how you are acting. This process requires vulnerability and the occasional admission that we don't have it all together, that we could have done better, or that we are the problem. This humbling concession is often what we need before we are willing to make meaningful change in order to show up better. However, if self-awareness is so valuable then why do so many people avoid doing this work? I believe it is because they are afraid of what they are going to see when they look in the mirror; therefore, it is easier to criticize and judge others than to look at your own reflection.

Ego hates vulnerability because it cannot survive in that condition. Vulnerability challenges you to glance in the rear-view mirror and see what you left behind. It is only then you will see the damage you caused, and the patterns of behavior that got you into the mess you're in. Be warned: your ego will work very hard to put you in the driver's seat and tell you, "Never look back. You're not going that way." This advice is misguided. Our self-awareness is a result of our ability to slow down long enough to look at ourselves and acknowledge how our actions are either empowering or derailing us personally and professionally. It is only then we can step back into the truth of who we are and experience life differently.

Ego is a malignancy on your awareness because it takes everything personally and then challenges you to defend your position. It flings your rational thinking out the window and then invades your body language, word choice, perspective taking, and ability to handle stress. When this happens, you become unaware of how your actions are impacting others.

Your growth fundamentally lies in your ability to look in life's rear-view mirror and make thoughtful choices about how you want to move forward in the next part of your journey. If you keep experiencing the same patterns along the way, then the issue is you and your inability to recognize how you're contributing to the problem. Slow down. Remember the truth of who you are. And give yourself permission to take an occasional glimpse at that mirror.

EGO CAUSES YOUR LOVE TO COME OUT BACKWARDS

A sea of hands go up and I hear people shout, "Yes!" when I ask a room full of leaders, "How many of you feel that sometimes the people we treat the worst are the people we love the most?" I can relate. I have always believed that education is the way out of your current condition. Therefore, I have stressed the importance of education and going to college to my nieces. They both made a choice after high school not to attend college. The decision upset me because I believed they were setting themselves up for a harder life. I found myself in many of our conversations bringing up the topic over and over. One day my youngest niece said, "We get it! You want us to go to college. You've made your point. We listened and now we've made our choice. We need you to support us." It was the slap in the face I needed. She was right. I had been communicating from my ego and perpetually trying to prove to them why my view was the correct one. As a result, they felt shamed. I love them so much that I could not detach from what I believed was best for them and allow them the autonomy to experience life on their terms. Isn't that the essence of unconditional love? I was communicating my thoughts and feelings from the wrong place and with the wrong intention. As a result, my love came out backwards and I acted in ways that did not honor the relationships I hold so dearly.

Love is supposed to be supportive, trusting, kind, and unconditional. However, sometimes our actions do not align with those characteristics. When we are so attached to the outcomes we want, because we believe they are best, we sometimes yell, shame, question, and even criticize to try to make our point. We love so much that sometimes our actions are not loving. It is in these moments that our love comes out backwards and in ways that do not honor the truth of who we are and what we really feel. Our love most often comes out backwards when we are scared of other people's choices and we do not have the vulnerability and courage to tell them.

Your ego will always cause your love to come out backwards—especially with the people you love the most. This happens for three main reasons. Firstly, we become so attached to the outcome we think is best for others that we don't take the time to step back and respond objectively. Our beliefs come out as judgment and our body language comes out as intensity or passive aggression. Secondly, we do not hold ourselves to the same level of accountability in our personal lives as we do in our professional lives. Every relationship creates a dynamic early on, and you know within that dynamic what you can and cannot get away with. We manage our behavior more at work because we know there are consequences for not being a good team player, for bullying, or for flying off the handle at random times. There are conditions attached to the way you show up at work, so you act accordingly. We go home where people get the real, stripped-down, warts-and-all version of us. We take these individuals for granted, never considering that they won't be there tomorrow. Thirdly, when you feel vulnerable inside, but lack the emotional intelligence to communicate this feeling in a healthy way, you lash out—with little to no impulse control—thinking you can govern the outcome you want. This behavior only pushes people further away and you end up manifesting the very thing you tried so hard to avoid.

Your ego wants you to scream your thoughts, feelings, and opinions from the top of the mountain and as loudly as you can. But, as a good friend once told me, "Just because you have something to say doesn't mean it needs to be said." Our ego thrives on being right and it is only concerned with winning the immediate conversation. This often leads to a lack of impulse control which makes us blind to the long-term impact of our actions.

It takes courage to accept people where they are along their journey. Oftentimes, we want to save people from a path we don't understand or that we believe is not in their best interests. You cannot love people into your version of existence. Our job is to learn how to love people right where they are, unconditionally. Choosing to show up from

> You cannot love people into your version of existence.

a place of love versus fear is a daily vulnerable choice. It's cultivated with risks and rewards. It requires us to acknowledge that someone's journey is uniquely and perfectly theirs, filled with lessons and experiences they have to learn. It calls us to stand with people on their journey, without shaming them into taking a different route. It challenges us to own our truth but not at the expense of other people's truth. And it asks us to stop trying to make our journey other people's experience. Today, you will make a choice to either stand with people and embrace them where they are, or your love will come out backwards while you look down on them with judgment and justify it in the name of "love." What would the bold new you do?

EGO TURNS DENIAL INTO YOUR STRONGEST DEFENSE

I was teaching a leadership class at Villanova University when a woman raised her hand and explained how she did not like working with one particular guy and wondered what she could do differently. When I asked her why she struggled working with him she stated how his presence was not inviting, she felt he was critical and judgmental of her, and he was closed off to collaboration. I then asked her, "How much are you demonstrating the exact same behaviors when you walk into the meeting room?" She paused and then acknowledged that she was demonstrating the same behaviors in defense of what she believed she would encounter. Isn't it ironic that we often dismiss people or do not like them for the same reasons we exhibit ourselves? We show up and lead better when we pull ourselves out of the denial that the other person is the problem and take responsibility for our half of the relationship.

Your ego prevents you from standing in the truth and it turns denial into your strongest defense. It is denial, not other people, that holds you back from growing. This is because you become recalcitrant and you shift from accountability to blame. Brené Brown in her TED talk, "The Power of Vulnerability," describes blame as, "a way to discharge pain and suffering." When we are miserable on the inside, our ego will try to use blame to discharge that pain and unresolved emotions.

Denial allows you the freedom of inaction and to continue living in the status quo. For example, if I stay in denial about my partner cheating on me then I do not have to face the consequences of what that means for my life. I can avoid having hard conversations, taking a stand for my values, or having to renegotiate the relationship. If I can stay in denial about my child being gay then I do not have to face how that scares me. I don't have to question my faith or my ability to truly love unconditionally. If I can stay in denial about my patterns in every relationship then I do not have to address them and admit that I am part of the problem.

Denial is used as your shield to defend yourself from information you do not like or do not want to hear. When we have the courage to lay down our shield, we learn how to take care of ourselves and our relationships with others in healthier ways.

It is a trend in business to only focus on your strengths. Though there is an important message in that statement, it is often watered down so much that people take it as an excuse not to focus on the behaviors holding them back. Newsflash: organizations don't let people go because of their strengths. They let them go because individuals are in denial about how their derailing behaviors are impacting the business. You do not need to spend effort trying to turn your weakness into your strength. However, you should ensure that your weakness is not a derailing behavior that is eroding trust and influence. Your goal is to make your shortcomings invisible. You cannot do that when you lack self-awareness and are in denial.

EGO ERODES YOUR AUTHENTIC CONFIDENCE

When you don't know who you are, you will allow your ego to dictate your self-worth. And there is nothing more dangerous than your ego on the hunt to prove its worthiness. Ego pulls you out of your inner truth and meticulously tries to fool you into living up to the image it wants for you. You cannot authentically connect and collaborate when you are waging an internal war and fighting for your identity.

> There is nothing more dangerous than your ego on the hunt to prove its worthiness.

The best version of you—your higher self—already knows you are good enough. Your ego, however, lures you into putting your self-worth in external things. It will force you to carry around an invisible backpack into which you cram everything you use to feel validated and worthy: titles, financial status, accolades, beliefs. You lash out in defend-and-attack mode the moment you believe any of the contents in your backpack are in danger.

I coached a CEO who used his results to validate his self-worth. He became angry and hurt when he received criticism or what he perceived as judgment from others. As a result, he found himself trying to prove people wrong and justify his actions. After he had cooled down, he would internalize the criticism and wear it on his soul as a reminder of his "disappointment." He had worked so hard to prove to people how good a job he was doing that it was discouraging when they did not see him as the superstar he tried so hard to portray. You would think all the acknowledgment of his value would make him feel worthy and appreciated. However, the exact opposite happened. He stated that the praise actually made him feel alone and isolated. He felt like an impostor and thought others were going to find him out. He realized from our conversation that he was choosing to own the criticism and dismiss the appreciation he deserved and had worked for. When I asked him why he did that he responded by saying, "Because it would end the chaos story . . . And I know how to thrive in chaos. I have purpose there."

Chaos is derived from confusion and confusion often leads to breakdown. Imagine driving your car and being puzzled about what decision to make when merging onto a roundabout or figuring out what street to turn down in an area with a bunch of one-way streets. It only takes one moment of confusion to create life-altering consequences. The same is true for how we navigate through the world. The confusion of who you are will always break down your authentic confidence and there will be life-changing impacts when that happens.

David Marcum and Steven Smith, authors of the book *Egonomics*, said, "Leadership is best reserved for people who don't need positions of leadership to validate who they are." Your authentic confidence is a result of standing, humbly and unapologetically, in the truth of who you are, and accepting the rewards and consequences that come from standing there. Accolades are wonderful, but they do not make you more or less worthy. Authentically confident people do not need external factors to validate who they are. Authentic confidence, derived from the clarity of your purpose and values, will always sustain you and it will never require you to prove it to anyone.

SIX BOLD WAYS TO KEEP YOUR EGO IN CHECK

It takes awareness to understand what ego is and how it impacts your life, but it takes action to do something about it. I believe we all have ego. Ego itself is not the problem. It is one's lack of awareness about their ego that is the problem. This lack of awareness keeps them reacting either as a raging megalomaniac or a victim. The more aware we become, the more we can shorten the time we spend in that disconnected space. Below are six reminders that will help you get over yourself and keep your ego in check.

> Ego itself is not the problem. It is one's lack of awareness about their ego that is the problem.

DON'T DROWN QUIETLY

I went kayaking and paddleboarding at Lake Lanier in Georgia with some friends. While making our way out on the lake, one of our friends on the paddleboard lost her balance and fell into the cold water. We all turned around to make sure she was okay. What happened next surprised me! Our other friend said, "I'm going in, too!" and jumped off his paddleboard into the frigid water. He jumped in so the other individual wouldn't feel embarrassed. They both made their way back onto their boards and I turned to him and said, "That was really awesome of you! What you did was a beautiful demonstration of empathy." He looked at me and responded, "Well, some people's ego won't allow them to ask for help."

Can't we all relate to this? There have been moments in our lives when we should have asked for help but didn't. Isn't it interesting that so many of us, in our most vulnerable moments, make a choice to drown quietly?

I went swimming with dolphins in 2016 while visiting the Big Island of Hawaii. Now, you should know that I am not the best swimmer. I can manage enough to save my life for a few minutes, but I struggle treading water. The captain took us two hours out to sea before spotting the first pod of dolphins. We were all sitting on the back of the boat waiting for the command to go. No one was wearing a life jacket, so I assumed I didn't need one. I had a snorkel and flippers on. What could go wrong? All of a sudden, the captain yelled, "Go! Go! Go!" Everyone started jumping into the water. I followed them in with the best pencil jump you've ever seen! Everything was fine for a few minutes until water started to fill up my mask. The only way I knew to correct this problem was to tread water, lift the mask up so the water spilled out, and then tighten it from the back. Y'all, I looked calm above the water, but underneath I was running the 100 meters against Usain Bolt. I started to panic after a few unsuccessful attempts to correct the problem. I knew if I panicked too much I would be in danger, so I decided to go back to the boat. I turned around and my heart sank. The boat had to be at least a quarter of a mile away. Three choices flashed through my mind. One: make my peace and drown. Two: wave my hands violently in the air and get rescued. Three: attempt to do the elementary backstroke all the way back to the boat. I wasn't ready for option one. My ego would not allow me to do option two. Option three was my only viable choice. Luckily, I made it back to the boat—with the most awkward backstroke and floating technique you've ever seen—where I was able to surrender my ego long enough to ask the captain for a pool noodle. In hindsight, I realize how foolish I was to risk my life because of my pride. It taught me a valuable life lesson: sometimes you need to wave your arms. Make some noise! Refuse to drown quietly. Drowning quietly is a choice, and you always have the right to make a different decision.

Our authentic self is confident and not afraid to show vulnerability. However, when we step away from that version of ourselves we react out of fear. We could often save ourselves, our job, and our relationships if we just had the courage and willingness to ask for help. However, we typically don't for three main reasons:

1. We lack self-awareness and do not even realize we need help before it is too late.

2. We are so caught up trying to portray an image we want others to see.

3. We are afraid of what others will think or do as a result of our vulnerability.

Remember: if you are ever reprimanded or judged by a leader when asking for help then that is more about them than it is about you, and you should re-evaluate whether that's the type of leader you really want to follow. Great leaders will always throw you a lifeline when you need it; however, the first step in saving yourself is asking for help. Don't drown quietly.

DON'T BE AN ASSHOLE

I was so insecure with myself throughout my twenties that I masked my self-doubt with aggression and armor. I was a bully to myself. I never physically hurt anyone else, but my inability to love myself unconditionally led to me making partners feel alone, peers feel small, and strangers invisible. I used my career results to validate my self-worth, so I made sure to get them at any cost. The fact is, it cost me everything meaningful: trust, authentic relationships, influence, and my character. My recovery has been long and arduous, but it has taught me that *how* we get results is just as important as the results themselves.

I recently received an email from a leader who said he understood the value of authenticity and vulnerability in leadership, but then asked, "So, why do the assholes succeed?" Wow! What a transparent and honest question that we should be discussing more in every organization. We could talk about the meaning behind the word "success" (which we do in the chapter on Take Care of You, First) and debate that they really are not "successful" in life or in leaving a positive legacy. However, many people below them would view them as "successful" based on their position, income, and influence.

The truth is we have all seen many leaders with ego make it to the top of organizations. Their bravado makes them come across as assholes at times, and the people below them are left wondering how the organization rewarded behavior like that. Assholes often get away with their bad behavior because of two main reasons:

1. The organization values results over culture—regardless of all the fancy posters on the wall and lip service that comes from the executive leadership team.

2. They are narcissistic chameleons who look out for themselves and know how to strategically play people to their favor.

Direct reports and peers receive the brunt of their emotional terrorism because the asshole knows they can get away with it. They typically escape punishment from their bad behavior as long as they keep adding value to the business and making the job of their supervisor easier. It is not until their behavior becomes a problem to their supervisor, or a liability to the organization, that leadership acknowledges and addresses their cockamamie behavior.

Working with these individuals is difficult, but my best advice is to focus on what you can control and let go of what you cannot. Therefore, here are five steps to dealing with assholes at work:

1. Stop trying to prove you are worthy of their kindness. *You will never win.*

2. Refuse to own their insecurity. *Their actions have nothing to do with you.*

3. Be direct (with tact) about their behavior while explaining the impact it has. *Turn the mirror on them.*

4. Be selective about who receives your time and energy. *Invest in those who value you.*

5. Show them the compassion they cannot offer you. *Someone once did that for you and it made all the difference.*

"WHY DO ASSHOLES SUCCEED?"

I asked my social media tribe why they believe assholes succeed. Below are some of their responses. I feel they all add a different level of insight.

W. O.

Because most people are too afraid to stand up to assholes. And they subconsciously enter into a Stockholm syndrome-like relationship where they enable the asshole by trying hard to please them in the hope that they'll be treated better.

C. H.

Do they really succeed, or is it an illusion of success?

J. G.

Because they are great self-promoters. Friendly people think more modestly and oftentimes care about others before themselves. It also could be that successful jerks stand out because they annoy our sense of justice, while successful friendly people are often taken for granted and overlooked for promotions.

J. K.

In my opinion, poor managers succeed in some organizations because they have yet to put equal value on the "what" and the "how." When a company has good people practices, and provides the opportunity for a performance calibration process, it is hard for the jerks to survive. So, valuing how things get done and allowing a safe place for varied points of view in an individual's performance is required. I'd also plug feedback tools like 360 and engagement surveys. Having said all that, these practices must be supported at the senior levels and you need a strong HR leader to hold them accountable.

M. M.

I believe assholes get what they deserve at some point.

J. I.

I think this depends on how we define success. If success is merely title, vertical momentum, or impressive business results then I agree—assholes can and do succeed. Bullies can achieve all of the "successes" above. However, what they don't have/get is influence, a followership, the ability to inspire and change the hearts and minds of people and companies, the title of leader, or a high level of respect and admiration. Those things would be on my list of what defines success—even if it costs me a promotion or title.

STOP TRYING TO ALWAYS LEAD THE BOAT

Great leaders know there is a time to lead the boat and a time to row the boat. They understand you cannot do both at the same time because you navigate on the level of your perspective. One of the many problems with ego is that it fools you into believing the boat is constantly sinking. As a result, you either show up as the hero because you believe you are the only one who can save it, or you spend every day buckled into your life jacket complaining about how the boat is going down. Either response only makes people want to throw themselves off the side of the boat and take their chances.

Your ability to lead the boat requires you to stand with the people who are rowing, but to have the discernment to zoom out and see what they cannot see, anticipate what they cannot anticipate, and ensure they are set up for success.

More specifically, leading the boat requires you to:
1. Discuss and align your crew with a vision.
2. Ensure your team has the resources and knowledge to accomplish this vision.
3. Remove any obstacles as quickly as possible.
4. Recognize the team.
5. Provide ongoing feedback and coaching to maximize performance.
6. Knock anyone out of the boat who tries to sink it.
7. Burn the boat once you get where you are going.

Rowing the boat requires you to:
1. Buy into the vision that has been established.
2. Focus on how you are rowing.
3. Be open to feedback and coaching.
4. Get results with integrity.
5. Contribute to the bigger picture.

High performing teams understand the differences in these roles, and they honor each person for the part they play in contributing to the overall success of the team. Every team needs someone leading the boat and other people rowing. Dysfunction happens the moment everyone on a team is rowing or when multiple people are trying to lead the boat in different directions.

Being a great leader of yourself is accepting there is a time to lead the boat and a time to row the boat. Your job is to know which part you are needed to play and contribute to your fullest potential. Your ego is always the captain of a one-man boat. Your best self is always a team player.

STOP TRYING TO OWN THE ROOM

We've all heard it before. A high-potential associate or new manager is being coached on the importance of confidence and presence, and then they're told that classic line, "Walk in and own the room." Please, *stop* saying this. It's awful advice!

Firstly, if the individual already knew how to "own the room" then they would. Secondly, your definition of "owning the room" is probably different from their interpretation, so without clarity as to how you define that phrase you leave them stranded—searching for some type of magical map to help them navigate their way. Thirdly, if someone lacks self-esteem then what they hear with that advice is, "fake it until you make it," so you teach them to put on a bunch of masks to try and prove they belong. As a result, they often lose their authentic self and their ability to genuinely connect with others.

Finally, it perpetuates an underlying problem in many organizations today: ego. We have enough egocentric leaders in the workplace who always shine the spotlight on themselves, fail to take other people with them when making decisions, believe their truth is the only truth, and are unconscious to the impact their presence has on others.

There is a different way, a better way, to coach your next generation of leaders. Instead of telling them to own the room, we should empower them to "own their energy." You might initially think the difference is just semantics, but I assure you, from my experience developing and coaching thousands of leaders in various industries, this distinction changes the way they communicate, connect to, and influence others.

Owning your energy requires you to take full responsibility for the mindset and presence you show up with every day. You are not worried about playing the starring role in the entire room, but you are committed to playing the starring role in your own life when it is your time to speak and contribute.

The best way we can coach someone to own their energy and act like they belong is by asking them to recall a time they felt proud of how they showed up. Give them the space they need to think through this and answer. After they tell you their story, ask them what specific actions made them feel so successful. Acknowledge their response and confirm that if they did it before then they already know how to use those traits to show up their best. Ask them how they could call on those same actions to show up their best in their next opportunity.

STAY CURIOUS

We approach life differently when we come from a place of curiosity. I saw a little girl, no more than six years old, running down the John Wayne Airport in Santa Ana, California. Her mother was trying to keep up with her, but the girl was jumping up and down with a look of amazement on her face. She turned around with the biggest grin and held up three fingers. She yelled, "It's three... I see three!" referring to their gate number. This little girl reminded me how important it is to stay curious in life and how our curiosity leads to our joy.

Persian poet, Rumi, has a famous line where he says, "Sell your cleverness and buy bewilderment." All of us would be better leaders at work and in our relationships if we applied this piece of wisdom. I interpret his use of the word "cleverness" as "wisdom." We spend so much time acquiring wisdom throughout our lives, and our ego gets addicted to our desire to prove our wisdom to others. When this happens, we are quick to respond, we only see things as black and white, we forfeit other people the right to share their cleverness, and we find ourselves in constant competition with each other's cleverness until someone loses.

Bewilderment is defined as the feeling of being perplexed and confused. In this state we have the opportunity to listen deeper, ask better questions so we can seek clarity, and challenge our preconceived notions. However, these feelings can often be uncomfortable, so your ego will force you to get out of them as quickly as possible.

We fundamentally show up differently when we come from a place of curiosity. When we sit back, and resist the desire to be right or critical, we become more open-minded and see things we would not have seen before. When we let go of the need to prove we belong, we give ourselves permission to sell a little bit of our cleverness so we can buy a little more bewilderment. Our ability to stay curious long enough and ask questions like, "I wonder why they believe what they do?" or "How would this work if . . . ?" or "What does this situation teach me about myself?" is why we become better leaders.

IN A WORLD FULL OF PEACOCKS, BE AN ELEPHANT

You know a peacock when you see a peacock. These individuals vie for attention and need to prove themselves, so they show up in ways that are excessive. Peacocks, in the animal kingdom, fan their beautiful and ornate trains during mating season. The males are demonstrating to the peahens how deserving and attractive they are. Humans aren't that much different. Hell, sometimes we are the peacock. We yell to make sure others hear us. We wear one too many statement pieces to stand out. We wear little or nothing at all so we don't become invisible. We shame other people to prove our views are the right ones, and we take up a lot of space so people notice we have arrived.

Perhaps we peacocks need to take a cue from elephants when it comes to how we show up in the world. The matriarch of the herd can teach us a lot about leadership and how to act like we belong versus trying to prove it. The matriarch is extremely influential. She demonstrates high levels of emotional intelligence and strategic decision-making during crises. The herd respects and relies on her leadership skills for their survival. These females are very compassionate animals that look out for the well-being of other elephants, and not just themselves. They feel emotion, show empathy, and they are resilient in the face of setbacks. The matriarch demonstrates quiet confidence, but she is not afraid to stand her ground when necessary. She is an example of how to lead with both head and heart.

In a world full of peacocks, be an elephant!

AFFIRMATION

Today, I let go of who I think I should be, and I give myself radical permission to be who I am. I acknowledge that the best version of myself does not require permission or approval from anyone else, so I surrender any need to try and prove myself. I will stand in the inner truth of who I am, unapologetically. When I do that, I feel more connected to myself and others. I feel strong in mind and humble in heart. I feel empowered to lead and communicate in ways that continuously bring out the best in me and others. Today, I am going to stand in my personal power and make my mark from the inside out.

CHAPTER THREE
LEADERSHIP SUMMARY

- Energy is about the mindset and presence you show up with every day.

- You experience life based on the level of your energy, and your energy dictates your ability to form trust, develop meaningful relationships, and cultivate authenticity.

- If you want to change how you lead your life then you must be awake to the energy level you are showing up in, understand core actions associated with each of the three energy levels, and take intentional steps to live at the energy level you desire.

3

want to be a great leader of yourself?

TAKE RESPONSIBILITY FOR YOUR ENERGY

Life changes when you
Take responsibility
For your energy.

I was contacted by a doctor in 2017 who wanted to work on raising his energy level because he was witnessing the negative impact it was having on himself and others. He told me, during our initial sessions, he was a "glass half empty" type of person. He lived in fear of being the dictatorial type of boss he used to be—so much so that he swung to the other extreme. As a result, people were taking advantage of him, not following through on their commitments, and he often found himself frustrated. After four months of coaching, I heard a different man start to show up to our calls. I acknowledged the difference and asked him what the catalyst for his change had been. He said, "You gave me some 'tough love' and it woke me up. You told me to stop making everything about me and asked, 'What would have to happen for you not to live your life as a victim?' It was then I decided to make a conscious choice on how I show up."

When this doctor decided to take responsibility for his energy, the universe responded in kind. He was more attentive to how he entered the workplace, how he chose to collaborate and bring other people with him, and he stopped wearing other people's negative energy as a symbolic badge that he had done something wrong. As a result, the energy of others and the energy in his practice started to change.

WHAT IS ENERGY AND WHY IS IT IMPORTANT?

The word "energy" is very ambiguous and many interpret it as being the "cheerleader" in the room. Though I think there is a time and place to champion others, I don't want us to confuse one's external display of emotions and feelings as the definition for energy, because what is going on inside has just as much to do with our energy as what people see on the outside. Energy is both the mindset and presence you show up with every day. Said differently: Energy = Mindset + Presence.

Energy =
Mindset +
Presence.

It is the energy you choose to show up with—whether conscious or subconscious—that impacts the quality of your relationships, and the quality of your relationships impacts your level of influence and credibility. Your energy directly correlates to how you go about getting results and the words people use to describe your character and legacy. Therefore, leaders have no greater obligation—for themselves, for others, and for the organization—than to take responsibility for their energy.

ENERGY = MINDSET

Mindset is a key ingredient that determines your overall energy as a leader. Carol Dweck, author of the book *Mindset: The New Psychology of Success*, spent years researching how someone's mindset impacts their success. She discovered that there are two distinctly different mindsets: fixed mindset and growth mindset. She says, "The view you adopt for yourself profoundly affects the way you lead your life. It can determine whether you become the person you want to be and whether you accomplish the things you value." If we want to play at the level of our potential, then we must make an intentional choice on the mindset we own—especially in life's most challenging moments.

"So, what do you want to get out of our time together?" I asked a client. She said, "I want to learn how to be in relationships where I do not exhaust people." She had found herself fired from jobs, not following through with commitments, and creating transactional relationships throughout much of her life. Her mindset played a key role in the dysfunction she was accumulating. She was always critical of herself and others, dissatisfied with the job she was in, placing unrealistic expectations on herself and others, and talking more than she was listening. As a result, she did not know or understand how to change her mindset to cultivate healthier relationships.

This client demonstrated classic signs of being an individual with a fixed mindset. Individuals with a fixed mindset are focused on winning and trying to prove themselves to the world. They believe their intelligence is static, which leads them to avoid challenges. Fixed-mindset people tend to ignore feedback and only want to be part of things that showcase their brilliance. Therefore, they do whatever it takes to protect their ego. They view imperfections as shameful, so these individuals are sensitive to setbacks and challenges.

Individuals with a growth mindset respond differently. They believe their intelligence can be developed, so they embrace challenges as opportunities to learn and grow. They are focused on achievement and gaining knowledge—especially in the face of adversity. Failure does not define this individual, so they use the experience to shape the person they can become. They learn from criticism and are resilient in life. They choose to convert setbacks into future success.

Carol Dweck says people get to make a choice of the type of relationships they want: "ones that bolster their egos or ones that challenge them to grow." That distinct mindset difference impacts how leaders cocreate relationships and build a culture either at work or at home. We spend a lot of time in organizations cultivating leaders' technical competence; however, we generally do not let people go because of ability issues. People are generally let go because of character issues. Character issues are always a result of the mindset someone owns. If we spent just as much time in organizations helping to foster and develop the mindset of our leaders as we did their technical competence, I believe we would create a better experience for everyone.

ENERGY = PRESENCE

The second key ingredient that shapes your overall energy is your presence. Presence deals with the verbal and nonverbal intensity you use to communicate. It is about knowing when to show up with strength and confidence and when to show up collaborative and empathetic. It takes strong emotional intelligence for you to not only be aware of your presence, but to know how to manage it. Individuals who take responsibility for their presence use their body language to make it safe for people to tell them the truth, and they know how to flex their style to meet people where they are. As a result, they inspire commitment from others, not just compliance.

I had the opportunity to sit down and talk with Melissa Lora, Taco Bell's former President of International Business, and I asked her, "What is one of the biggest factors that holds leaders back?" Without hesitation, she indicated that it was intensity. She defined intensity as being so focused on your agenda that you are unaware or uninterested in how your presence is impacting others on the team. She said, "These leaders become so attached to the outcome they desire that they do not sit back and create space in meetings to activate others' brilliance. Their energy heats up the room and everyone can feel it. Intensity intimidates people out of their best thinking. It can erode influence and trust. Because they are so focused on "the pitch" they are trying to make, they forget who is on their team and how collectively they may innovate to create a better outcome. As a result, everyone loses. Collaboration, creativity, innovation, and productivity are all sacrificed."

Intensity intimidates people out of their best thinking.

74

We have all heard the classic line, "It's not what you say, it's how you say it." The reason we hear it so much is because it's true. There is even science to back it up. We now know from research in neuroscience that the brain responds very differently when it senses fear versus safety. This all has to do with the intensity of our presence. Our body releases oxytocin, the "trust hormone," when the environment we are in elicits safety. This chemical effect is what allows people to feel connected, to listen, and to collaborate. However, our brain is hardwired to always scan the environment for threats. When it perceives danger, it releases cortisol, the "stress hormone," into the body. This is your body's natural defense mechanism to make you stop and—like Whoopi Goldberg in the movie Ghost—say, "Molly, you in danger, girl!" It is in these moments that we step out of our personal power and revert to our biological fight-or-flight response. When this happens, people can no longer hear what we are trying to communicate, and our influence is diminished.

Taking responsibility for your energy is being awake and accountable to both your mindset and presence. It is understanding that your energy is the foundation for how you lead, love, and communicate in every aspect of your life. Now, let's explore the three different energy levels and the core actions associated with each.

> Taking responsibility for your energy is being awake and accountable to both your mindset and presence.

THE THREE CORE ENERGY LEVELS WE ALL SHOW UP IN

After working with thousands of leaders in different countries and across various industries, I have noticed consistent patterns in how they show up and get results. I have analyzed those patterns and outlined three core energy levels. I have used this model within small businesses and Fortune 500 organizations to help leaders shift their energy and improve organizational and team culture.

I have categorized the three levels of energy as basement, lobby, and penthouse. This is important because you lead and experience life on the level of your energy. The higher up you go, the more you have access to seeing, and when we see clearer we make very different choices. It is important to note that we go through all three energy levels from time to time; however, our ability to be awake to which energy level we are in most often, and the rewards and consequences associated with it, makes all the difference.

I will define the core leadership style, emotion, and most common actions associated with each level of energy. Review the three different levels, be honest with yourself about which level you show up in most often, and consider what you need to do differently so you can honor the bold new you you're becoming.

Remember: you are experiencing life on the level of your energy. That is a choice, and you can make a different one at any moment!

LEVEL ONE ENERGY: BASEMENT

Javier walked into his team meeting and sat down. He was the type of individual who always told people he valued their ideas and wanted their thoughts on how to take the team and business to the next level. However, he started most conversations by sharing his thoughts first and then criticizing anyone with a different opinion. Javier was so caught up in being right and leading people to the solution he wanted, he could not hear what other people were trying to say. People often felt dismissed by him, so they checked out. His intensity was not worth their energy. Javier left the meeting feeling it was successful and that expectations were clear. He was unable to see how his intensity got in the way of his ability to take people with him and gain buy-in. He, like many leaders, sacrificed relationships with people for self-validation and a desire to drive results.

I refer to individuals who show up in level one energy as "Basement Dwellers." This is not one of those highfalutin basements that is bigger and nicer than some people's entire home. This is the kind of dilapidated basement you see in horror movies. This environment has a few defining characteristics that impact the occupant's behavior. The look of a basement is usually dark which results in limited and obstructed vision. Their truth is only based on what they can see, and, since their sight is restricted, they tend to have a very narrow-minded view of the truth. They create a lot of stories and assumptions based on no facts or the facts they have cherry-picked for their argument. It is often cold in the basement, which leads to isolation and detachment. Intimacy cannot thrive in a space where there is no warmth. The space is often confined and uncomfortable. People do not want to be in the basement, but they do not know how to get out, so they learn to thrive in the dysfunction they are in.

Individuals in the basement lead mostly from their head-space, and their actions and choices are rooted in fear. They have put their value in their ability to drive results—at any cost—and they have adopted a transactional leadership style. Many of their actions are entrenched in their ego and they are often unaware of the impact their behavior has on others. The most common action I see at this level is judgment and criticism. Efficiency and effectiveness are important for these individuals, so they easily detach from relationships when they feel disappointment or when someone does not live up to their expectations. These leaders coach others and participate in meetings that feel scripted and inauthentic. They lack flexibility in the present moment because they are so caught up in driving towards where they want to be in the future. If leaders who demonstrate predominately level one energy are in organizations that only value results, they typically excel and are rewarded for this behavior. As a result, they get compliance from their team, but they never get commitment.

I went to an organization to speak on the key drivers of employee engagement and how to ignite the best in people. The executive leadership team was conducting a recognition ceremony before my presentation, so I sat towards the front and participated in the celebration. However, a short time later, I became concerned about the message these leaders were sending to the organization. In preparation for my meeting I had analyzed all the employee engagement results and knew how these employees felt about their direct supervisors. I was watching the recognition ceremony and witnessing the managers with the lowest engagement scores get rewarded in front of their peers for having the best results. These managers had produced great results that year, but they did it by bullying, not leading and taking others with them, and teams were miserable. The leadership group had spent the whole morning talking about how valuable people were in the organization and then went against everything they said when handing out the awards.

Time after time, I see leaders stand up and talk about the importance of putting people first, but then they make decisions and implement processes that go directly against that philosophy. Organizations reward bad behavior when they only hold individuals accountable for results and not how they get results. When your organization is solely focused on the end result, you create a transactional culture where people are sacrificed for numbers. Some of the core actions associated with that basement-level mindset are included in Figure 1.1.

CHARACTERISTICS OF LEVEL ONE ENERGY

3 LEVELS OF ENERGY — **LEVEL ONE** BASEMENT *DWELLERS*

CORE LEADERSHIP STYLE	Transactional
CORE FOCUS	Results
CORE EMOTION	Fear
CORE ACTIONS	<ul><li>Listens to be Right</li><li>Critical & Judgmental</li><li>Puts Value in Competence</li><li>Lacks Self-Awareness</li><li>Creates Lots of Stories</li><li>Mircromanages/Controls</li><li>Takes No Accountability</li><li>Intensity Holds Them Back</li><li>Lacks Impulse Control</li></ul>
ADVANTAGE	Get Immediate Results
DISADVANTAGES	<ul><li>Sacrifice Relationships</li><li>No Buy-In From Team</li></ul>

Figure 1.1

I coached a leader who was valued in the organization for his competence, but he struggled with how he developed authentic relationships. The more we talked, the more I realized his transactional approach to relationships was a result of what he believed about himself. He admitted that when he started to lack confidence and not feel "good enough" in any situation, he would jump straight into "fix it" mode because fixing things made him feel valuable and worthy. However, the consequence was that it cost him intimacy in most of his relationships, which led to a lack of trust. He started making different choices when he learned that fear was driving his behavior and that specific actions were holding him back from being the type of leader he said he wanted to be.

Harvard Business Review asked the question, "Is it better to be loved or feared?" in their 2013 article "Connect, Then Lead." The research proved that both fear (defined as strength, agency, or competence) and love (defined as warmth, communion, and trustworthiness) are both important, but love needs to come before strength. They emphasized, "Leaders who project strength before establishing trust run the risk of eliciting fear, and along with it a host of dysfunctional behaviors. Fear can undermine cognitive potential, creativity, and problem solving, and cause employees to get stuck and even disengage."

It is someone's inability to see how their actions are impacting those around them that keeps them playing smaller than their potential. Everyone suffers when leaders, like Javier, are allowed to get away with behavior that does not honor the best of them or the organization. We all go to level 1 energy from time to time, but we must be aware of when we are there and make a conscious choice to pull ourselves higher. Organizational culture and relationship trust cannot thrive in this environment in the long term. Persian poet Hafiz once said, "Fear is the cheapest room in the house. I'd like to see you living in better conditions."

LEVEL TWO ENERGY: LOBBY

Sara and her husband had experienced communication issues for a year. They had gotten so busy being busy that they forgot to make time for each other. When they did spend time together, it usually ended up in an argument. Sara loved her husband and realized if she wanted their marriage to work, she had to stop coming from a place of fear. She made a choice to start showing up differently in how she approached their arguments. She allowed her husband space in the conversation to express his thoughts without interrupting him—even when she did not agree. She was intentional about making her body language appear collaborative and empathetic. She knew if they did not feel safe in the conversation then neither of them would be as transparent as they needed to be to work through their issues. She knew she could not change what had happened in the past, but she could control her response moving forward. She took accountability for her part in the relationship, apologized for letting him down, and together they renegotiated what they needed from each other and how they could show up better. Slowly, and over time, their relationship improved.

I refer to individuals who show up in level two energy as "Lobby Listeners." The lobby of a hotel is brighter than the basement, more comfortable to be in, and is occupied by more people who are collaborating and engaging in conversations. Lobby Listeners are driven by empathy and lead mostly from their heart-space. They believe the way to get long-term, sustainable results is through people, so their main focus is on building genuine relationships and influence. As a result, their core leadership style is participative. They are good listeners, show up fully present for others, and are intentional about making deposits into people's emotional bank accounts. Therefore, they typically earn commitment from their direct reports and have deep relationships with the people in their life. Figure 1.2 highlights the core actions associated with Lobby Listeners.

CHARACTERISTICS OF LEVEL TWO ENERGY

3 LEVELS OF ENERGY	♡ LEVEL TWO LOBBY LISTENERS
CORE LEADERSHIP STYLE	Participative
CORE FOCUS	Relationships
CORE EMOTION	Empathy
CORE ACTIONS	• Listens to Understand • Question Own Assumptions • Developing Self-Confidence • Aware of Behavior & Impact • Slows Down / Creates Space • Makes Emotional Deposits • Takes People With Them • Practices Forgiveness • Takes Accountability
ADVANTAGE	Get Buy-In & Commitment
DISADVANTAGES	• Can Lack Assertiveness • Don't Uphold Accountability

Figure 1.2

TAKE RESPONSIBILITY FOR YOUR ENERGY

My favorite quote of all time comes from Oprah Winfrey. I believe this one quote has the power to radically change how people show up and communicate if they apply it to their lives. Oprah says, "Every single person you meet shares a common desire. They want to know: Do you see me? Do you hear me? Does what I say mean anything to you?" Our ability to make people feel seen and heard, especially in the difficult moments, determines the type of leader we are in this world. The core actions of a leader with level two energy are what makes someone feel seen and heard.

A woman raised her hand during one of my workshops in San Antonio, Texas. She asked, "I only lead from my head-space, so how do I add just a little more heart?" We all found the humor in her desire to only add "a little more heart" (level two energy) to the way she leads, but you have to start somewhere. I told her the place to start is by putting the relationship with the individual before the result you want. I then asked the room, "What would we do differently as leaders if we put the focus on relationships, instead of just the end result?" Someone yelled, "I wouldn't go around the individual even though it might be easier. I would talk to them directly and allow them to resolve the issue." Someone else mentioned how they would take the time to listen and really try to understand their point of view. Other ideas were acknowledging people for their contributions, celebrating milestones, becoming better at small talk, and taking a personal interest in people. There is no one right action on how to add more heart into your leadership approach, but putting relationships before results is a great place to start.

Finally, Lobby Listeners must be careful they don't lead so much from only their heart-space that they get sucked into other people's drama, don't say the things they need to say, and don't hold others accountable to defined expectations. Remember: you can be empathetic while still holding others accountable. Making someone feel seen and heard does not mean you remove responsibility from them or yourself. The ability to lead and communicate from both your head and your heart is what defines leaders who show up in the penthouse.

LEVEL THREE ENERGY: PENTHOUSE

Susan had a direct report who was struggling. They had previously undergone several coaching conversations, but she did not feel like the direct report understood the seriousness of the issue. Susan believed in this individual and was committed to having one more conversation—even though her boss thought she should let him go. Susan called Mark into the office and shared her truth about his actions and the impact they were having on everyone else. She balanced the seriousness of the conversation with the intensity of how the message was delivered. Mark apologized for his behavior and acknowledged he didn't realize his actions were causing any problems. Susan expressed her belief in Mark and said she would have his back if he was willing to do the necessary work to turn things around.

Leaders who show up in level three energy, who I call "Penthouse Visionaries," experience life and relationships on a different level. The penthouse is full of windows and light, which allow you to stay focused on the big picture, and the 360-degree view reminds you of all the choices you have available. These individuals operate on a higher level of awareness and emotional intelligence than people in the lower levels of energy. They are impeccable leaders of themselves because they know who they are. This knowledge is the catalyst for their authentic confidence. They focus on building trust with others because they understand that's how you forge meaningful relationships, influence, and credibility. Their choices and actions are rooted in love—first for themselves and then for others. Authenticity is a value for these people and they foster a culture where others feel they can show up as their authentic self everywhere they go. They are no longer trying to prove to others how talented, smart, and valuable they are because they have a strong sense of self-worth. Their self-confidence comes from being driven by purpose, not titles. These are some of the best leaders and they understand that great leadership is about leading with both your head and heart. They are intentional about creating win-win opportunities for the organization, the people working there, and customers. As a result, they have transformative cultures that exceed people's expectations. Figure 1.3 summarizes the core actions associated with Penthouse Visionaries.

CHARACTERISTICS OF LEVEL THREE ENERGY

3 LEVELS OF ENERGY

LEVEL THREE
PENTHOUSE
VISIONARIES

CORE LEADERSHIP STYLE	Transformational
CORE FOCUS	Trust
CORE EMOTION	Love
CORE ACTIONS	• Listens to Connect • Demonstrates Compassion • Values Authenticity / Purpose • High Emotional Intelligence • Transparent With People • Focuses on Opportunity • Honors Boundaries • Recognizes Others • Focuses on the Big Picture
ADVANTAGE	High Levels of Credibility
DISADVANTAGES	• Perceived Overly Positive • Out of Touch with Reality

Figure 1.3

The single most important piece of advice I've ever received, and that changed the trajectory of my career, was from Greg Creed, CEO of Yum! Brands. He was talking with a group of leaders I was coaching at Taco Bell when someone asked, "What career advice would you offer us?" His response created palpable silence in the room. He said with humility, "Stop trying to prove you belong, and act like you belong." Leaders who show up in the penthouse are no longer trying to prove themselves to anyone. They already believe they belong and that their presence adds value.

Leaders who show up in level three love themselves and others enough to be direct and unapologetic with their boundaries. They are clear about what is okay and what is not okay, so everyone is playing by the same rules. There are times when honoring their boundaries isn't going to make other people happy, isn't going to feel comfortable, and isn't going to make them "liked." However, after working with leaders who show up with deep levels of authenticity and boundary-setting, I know they would say, "I am not here to be liked; I am here to be kind. Being liked is a desire of my ego. Being kind is a product of my character, and being kind does not require other people's approval." You cannot expect others to honor your boundaries when you don't honor them yourself. Honoring your boundaries is a way for you to respect yourself, communicate with transparency how you expect to be treated, and prevent yourself from ever settling for less than you deserve.

The core actions associated with people who show up with level three energy are what it takes to foster trust. When we do not trust someone, it is because we do not trust their intent. We question the motives behind their actions based on what we feel and what we have experienced in the past. Building trust is the foundation for every healthy relationship. It requires us to be both transparent and truthful with our intentions. When we are not, people create a story about our motives, and that story is always grounded in fear. Your relationships cannot survive people's unresolved fear-stories. The anecdote is transparency and truth. Harvard Business Review's research states, "Trust provides the opportunity to change people's attitudes and beliefs, not just their outward behavior. That's the sweet spot when it comes to influence and the ability to get people to fully accept your message."

Finally, Penthouse Visionaries are not living in some fantasyland where everything is happy all the time. These individuals are not immune to heartache, frustration, or from finding themselves in the basement. The difference is how they respond. When leaders who resonate with predominately level three energy find themselves in the basement, they allow themselves to feel what they need to feel, but then they get to a point where they say, "How do I grow from this experience? How do I become better because of what happened to me, not despite it?" They acknowledge their experiences without indulging them. Their perspective allows them to see all the options and opportunities available, and they make choices that bring them back to the penthouse. The penthouse requires leaders to own a growth mindset.

⋮ DOWNLOAD A COPY OF THE THREE ENERGY LEVELS ⋯⋯⋯⋯
Sometimes it is easier to see the three energy levels side by side. You can download a summary of all three levels at boldnewyou.com.

MOVING FROM FEAR TO LOVE

Whether it is renowned psychiatrist Elisabeth Kübler-Ross or various spiritual teachings, many people have said that love and fear are the two core emotions. Every other feeling is an outgrowth of one of them and it is impossible to experience both simultaneously. We create more clarity in our lives when we understand that love and fear are driving our choices and we get to choose which one of them serves our higher self. Understanding this concept does not mean we avoid feeing the emotions connected with fear. All emotions aid in your growth and teach you what you need to learn about yourself. What it does is allow you to slow down, acknowledge what you're feeling, identify the underlying causes triggering those feelings, and give you the awareness to move through them in a much healthier way instead of emotionally disconnecting. Your ability to pause before you react is at the heart of your ability to shift from fear to love.

A client of mine worked for 12 hours before coming home to his wife and newborn baby. The moment he walked in the door, his wife handed him the baby and said, "Here. I need a break." The husband understood the pressures of a stay-at-home mom and how that role can make you feel isolated and with little time for yourself. He spent the next three hours taking care of his baby boy while his wife worked out, showered, and cooked dinner. When dinner was done, she wanted him to sit down and eat with her. He, however, wanted her to enjoy the meal while he took care of the baby and then they could trade off and he could take some time for himself. His wife insisted he eat with her. He could feel his blood start to boil. In that moment, he felt several emotions associated with fear: aggravation, irritation, and dismissal. All these feelings were causing him to detach and he was about to say something hurtful. As a result, he decided to pause and think about what was underlining these feelings. Instead of reacting from a place of fear, blowing up, and having to apologize for something he would regret, he decided to come from a place of love and be transparent about what he was feeling in the moment. He told her he felt aggravated because he had been going for over 15 hours. He understood she needed a break, so he jumped in to help her when he got home. But now, he needed some time to unwind and decompress and required her to be more understanding about his time and not just her own. She replied, "Wow! Who are you? Where did you learn that?" Pausing allowed my client to identify and accept his initial feelings, explore what was behind them, and then make a choice that came from a more loving place, that would move the relationship forward in a healthy way. His ability to demonstrate both empathy and transparency was only possible because he made a decision not to react from fear, but from a place rooted in love.

We often respond from a place of fear when we fail to pause, and we react without taking a moment to think about what we are really feeling and why. Phillip Moffitt, former CEO and Editor-in-chief of *Esquire*, summarized it best when he said, "Fear distorts what you see. It focuses primarily on the negative, exaggerates the potentially threatening, filters out alternative views, and causes you to compromise your core values out of the urgent need to survive. Fear when not named narrows your vision, shuts down intuition as well as common sense reflection, and promotes violent actions."

Moving from fear to love is a self-discovery journey, and the bridge that connects the two is empathy.

> Moving from fear to love is a self-discovery journey, and the bridge that connects the two is empathy.

Celebrity Trainer Bob Harper, in Season 14 of *The Biggest Loser*, was working with a contestant on the show named Gina who was overweight and paralyzed by fear. She had what many people would consider professional success, but she could not revel in it because of what she felt like on the inside. She was randomly selected on episode six to be the person whose weight would count that week for her entire team. The pressure and accountability were too much for her and she broke down. Bob looked right at her and said, "Don't come from a place of fear! Fear is the main problem that brought you here."

Fear drives all toxic behavior, so we must move past the idea that talking about and expressing emotions is "touchy-feely" stuff. It is this touchy-feely stuff that drives engagement, culture, retention, and an exceptional customer experience that impacts the bottom line of every business. This touchy-feely stuff allows you to provide unconditional love, cultivate intimacy in your relationships, make your child feel heard, and honor your intuition when you have walked away from who you say you are. Our inability to be comfortable talking about emotions keeps us playing smaller than our potential. Our desire to just "stick to the facts" prevents us from taking people with us along the journey, and is why we fail as leaders. Emotions are at the core of everything good and everything significant in business and relationships. You must learn to use emotions in a way that serves you and your relationships with others.

Here is my challenge to you. If you have a problem with the word "love," because of how you have chosen to define it, then replace it with the word "trust" because you can't have love without it. Trust is the key ingredient to loving wholeheartedly and unconditionally. Our ability to trust will never exceed our ability to love. Love removes judgment. Love creates clarity. Love breaks down barriers. Love shatters unrealistic expectations. Love honors accountability. Love forgives. Love extends second chances. Love gives people the space to dream bigger. Love challenges people to rise up to the level of their potential. In the end, those traits are always the most admired leaders and what prevents us from becoming a sleepwalker!

WHY SLEEPWALKERS ARE SO DANGEROUS

Ralph Ellison, in his book *Invisible Man*, says, "There are few things in the world as dangerous as sleepwalkers." I could not agree more. I define a sleepwalker as someone whose actions do not align with how they say they want to be perceived by others. Easily stated, they lack self-awareness. These individuals view themselves one way, but everyone else has a very different perception. I know you're thinking of someone that fits that description right now! These sleepwalkers stalk the halls of organizations, unconscious and blind to the impact their behavior has on a team, customers, and the relationships in their personal life. They often get results, but they sacrifice trust, engagement, and influence. They live and fester in the basement.

I recently worked with a senior executive who made it to the top levels of the organization because of his smarts, work ethic, and ability to get stuff done. However, in the pursuit of getting the work done he bullied others, had to be the smartest person in the room, failed to take people along the journey with him, and made people feel invisible.

He wanted to be a leader who was admired and respected, but the patterns of behavior he had learned and used to get results was creating the opposite impact. Furthermore, his organization—like many others—enabled his sleepwalking when they chose to ignore his behavior because of his capacity to drive strong results.

Sleepwalkers are so dangerous because they are not even aware they are sleeping. They have learned to lead, love, and communicate with their eyes closed for so long that they often do not know they can experience life differently. They toss around their words like they don't have an effect on people. They justify their present condition with, "This is just who I am!" They are blind to the fact that they keep themselves and others playing small.

The greatest gift you will ever give a sleepwalker is the gift of sight. To safely help a sleepwalker look at themselves in the mirror is one of the most rewarding and challenging experiences they will be given—even when they cannot appreciate it in the moment. We help sleepwalkers regain their vision when we appreciate them right where they are, shine light on their behavior, and love them enough to hold them accountable. Holding ourselves and others accountable starts with clarity on what you want your emotional wake to be.

WANT TO CHANGE YOUR ENERGY? START BY CHANGING YOUR EMOTIONAL WAKE.

It was the middle of winter in Denver, Colorado and I was heading to the warmth of my car like one of those early morning mall walkers, when, all of a sudden, I heard a sweet voice behind me say, "Excuse me, sir." I realized it was a homeless lady. I was so focused on myself and getting to my car that I chose to ignore her. Again, without ever raising her voice, she said, "Excuse me, sir." I kept walking. I had created a story in my head that all she wanted was money and I was not going to give her any. A third time, "Excuse me, sir." I stopped. I remember turning around and talking to this woman. To this day, I don't remember what we talked about or if I even gave her money, but what I do remember is getting to my car, sitting in the driver's seat with my hands on the wheel, and thinking about the number of times I had used my voice and presence to make another human being feel completely dismissed. I started to reflect on all the ways I make people feel invisible: not being fully present and listening, getting so busy that I do not take the time to properly thank them, dismissing their feelings or ideas. This woman transformed, in my eyes, from a homeless lady to my teacher, and she taught me a valuable lesson on why it is important to take responsibility for your energy. As a result, I never wanted to make another human being feel that way again.

Susan Scott discusses the impact of someone's emotional wake in her 2002 book, *Fierce Conversations*. Fundamentally, your emotional wake is the psychological ripple your presence leaves on people. That ripple is conscious or subconscious, positive or negative, promoting collaboration or defensiveness. Every choice you make—the words you use, the actions you take, what you post on social media—leaves an emotional imprint that stays with others long after you are gone. Part of being a great leader of yourself is being aware to the wake you are leaving and being intentional about the wake you want to leave. Without a vision, you have nothing to hold yourself accountable to and you will continue to sleepwalk. After my incident in Colorado, I made the commitment to show up more present, empathetic, and inspiring.

> Your emotional wake is the psychological ripple your presence leaves on people.

The emotional residue you leave on people is either building up or tearing down trust in every relationship. As David Horsager says in his book, *The Trust Edge*, "Trust, not money, is the currency in business and life." We spend a lot of time helping leaders build brands, but not nearly enough time helping them understand how their brand is cultivating trust.

Imagine yourself in your car, driving down the same road you drive every day to work while listening to your favorite artist. All of a sudden, you notice a new billboard up ahead on the right. As you get closer you start to laugh because you notice it is an abnormally large picture of you with the text, "I AM _____, _____, _____." As you drive past the billboard you reach down and turn off the radio and you start to reflect on those blank spots. You ask yourself, "What are the three words or phrases I want people to use when they think of me?"

Choosing the three words you hope people use when asked to describe you is important because it gives you a bold vision to hold yourself accountable to every day, and it acts as a filter for how you should manage your energy. I encourage you not to choose words that sound sexy or how you think other people want you to show up. I literally had a college athlete choose the words "BIG SEXY" in my workshop. Needless to say, he and I laughed and then we had a conversation about what his long-term goals were. Get clear on the standard for how you want to show up in all aspects of your life. Your three words should be the same personally and professionally. The beauty of being a better leader of yourself is that you give yourself radical permission to take off the mask you wear in all the areas of your life. Your emotional wake is your true north to living an authentic life.

IDENTIFY THE EMOTIONAL WAKE YOU WANT TO LEAVE ON OTHERS

When people talk about me, I hope they say I am:

_____   _____   _____

Next, identify 3-5 actions for each word that would promote your ability to be perceived as that word.

Every day you show up with no clear vision you sacrifice your impact—all in the name of good intentions. Good intentions are not enough. Transformational leaders take responsibility for the wake they leave on others. They have the self-awareness to create their vision and the self-management to live it out. Our desired emotional wake calls us to a higher standard of living. It requires us to take personal accountability for our thoughts and actions, and it uses every interaction as a masterclass to teach us about ourselves, our personal power, and the work we still have left to do. It is the first step towards taking responsibility for our energy.

In summary, we see and experience life based on the level of our energy; therefore, we have no greater obligation than to take responsibility for the energy we show up with every day. Taking responsibility for your energy does not mean you do not value results. It is a testimony to your belief that how you get results is just as important as the results themselves. Taking responsibility does not mean we are always going to get it right, but it is a commitment to ourselves that when we don't get it right we will slow down and make it right. If we want to live a happier life and lead better teams then we must raise the level of our energy, which requires us to move from fear to love. Everyone benefits when leaders take responsibility for the energy they show up with every day and when organizations hold them accountable for it.

TAKE RESPONSIBILITY FOR YOUR ENERGY

1. What energy level is demonstrated by most leaders in the organization?

2. What is the vision for how we want leaders to lead in the organization?

3. How do the processes we have in place enable or block our vision?

4. What expectations do we need to communicate across the organization?

5. How will we hold people accountable to these expectations?

6. What do we as a leadership team need to take responsibility for?

7. How are we currently rewarding bad behavior throughout the organization?

8. How much of the recognition we provide focuses on results versus the behaviors demonstrated to get the results?

9. How are we helping develop the character of leaders?

10. What recommendations would you make if you were a consultant brought into the organization to provide advice on how to develop better leaders?

ENERGY AFFIRMATION

Today, I choose what I see, and I choose to see the potential in myself and in others. I walk out into the world with my eyes wide open and with the ability to see the skills, passion, and dreams of what others have to offer. I acknowledge the incredible power my presence makes in this world and how, at any moment, I can use my presence to transform how others see themselves. I choose to use my presence to allow others the space to live unapologetically in their authenticity. My actions will be rooted in love and will inspire trust with others. And when the day is done, I will see myself differently because I know you can only extend to others the level of vision you offer to yourself. This is the person I want to be in the world. This is the person I am.

CHAPTER FOUR
LEADERSHIP SUMMARY

- We never lose our voice. We give it away when we lose the awareness of its power and we stop believing our voice means something.

- When you find your voice, you find your confidence.

- Owning your authentic voice starts by accepting and appreciating the voice you already have, realizing that it has been shaped by generations before you, and using it so you connect and impact others in meaningful ways.

- Every conversation matters, and this chapter will provide you with eight communication strategies you can apply to maximize your impact and credibility.

4

want to be a great leader of yourself?

OWN YOUR VOICE

Speak up. Own your voice.
What you have to say matters.
Silence is a choice.

I had a limited idea of what pageants were about until I joined the Miss Kentucky system and coached contestants before they headed to the national Miss America competition. The Miss America Organization taught me a valuable lesson about standing center stage and how important it is to own your voice right where you are.

Savannah Cooper was one of the young women I had the good fortune to see grow as she discovered her voice. Savannah was 15 years old when I met her, and her life is a testimony to what individuals living with chronic illness experience. She was diagnosed, at just seven years old, with tethered spinal cord syndrome and Ehlers-Danlos syndrome. As a result, she has endured multiple surgeries, testing, and medications. She has dealt with over 40 kidney infections in the past four years. These treatments have taken a toll on her body and caused her to lose her hair. Pageants allowed Savannah to surround herself with people who believed in her and encouraged her to be her authentic self—chronic illness and all. Therefore, before the evening gown competition at Miss Kentucky's Outstanding Teen, Savannah was struggling to decide whether to wear her wig. She explained how supportive everyone around her was and how their encouragement fueled her confidence. She made the decision to step out from behind the curtain and stand center stage without a wig. She noted, "It was a big step. It was a statement that this is who I am." That one decision and the support she received was a catalyst in helping Savannah find her authentic voice. She told me, "Everything spiraled afterwards." Savannah worked up the courage to post her first picture on social media showing her beautiful bald head. She was terrified. She had been bullied for looking different from others and she was expecting the worst. The opposite happened. People rallied around her, the comments were positive, and people were curious to learn more. Savannah launched a #SavStrong Instagram account which led to promoting patient advocacy. Savannah has now used her voice and platform to talk with doctors at the Cincinnati Children's Hospital and public schools, and she told me, "Using my voice is not about being liked or not liked. This is about me telling my story because I have a story to tell. I can inspire and educate others, so why not keep sharing it?"

So many people think once they become more confident they will start to speak up. It does not work that way! Savannah demonstrated that you find your courage when you feel fear, but step onto the stage anyway. If you want to discover your confidence, you must start by owning your voice. You do that in small meaningful moments—like the time you spoke up and shared with your partner how you really felt, the time you went to your boss and asked for what you wanted, the time you refused to allow your friend to take advantage of you, the time you defended the stranger on the street, the time you gave a presentation and didn't die, and the time you used your voice to make someone else feel less alone. Every one of those meaningful moments were a catalyst you needed for your growth, but it was up to you to lean into them.

When you find your voice, you find your confidence. And finding your voice requires you to stop searching for the voice you want and celebrate the one you already have. When you do this, you aren't afraid to have the conversations you need to have—even when they are uncomfortable. You speak up—even when it is not popular. You share your truth in a way that aligns with your character—so you refuse to own how other people interpret or respond to your thoughts and feelings. Finding your voice does not call for you to get all your words right, to say things the way you believe other people want you to say them, or to have a large platform before you start to share your message. It only challenges you to use the voice you have and stand center stage to share it. Standing center stage takes courage because it means you must believe your voice matters and that the world needs to hear your message, ideas, and thoughts in the way only you can say it.

> When you find your voice, you find your confidence.

SIX WAYS YOU GIVE YOUR VOICE AWAY

You lose your voice and forget what you are worth when you make the choice not to stand center stage in your life. When you forget what you are worth, you make yourself invisible to avoid standing out in the crowd. Instead of embracing being center stage, you choose to remain on the sidelines. People who stand on the sidelines are consumed with the possibility of "if": If people don't see me, they can't hurt me. If I don't speak up, people can't judge my thoughts or criticize the way I talk. If I don't ask for what I want, I don't have to face the possibility of rejection or embarrassment. If I don't go after my dreams, I don't have to be disappointed in myself if I fail. These individuals spend so much of their life trying to protect themselves from being hurt that they end up sabotaging themselves and their success. All they really want is for people to see them, but they never even show the world who they really are. Their actions make them invisible and the most people get to experience from them is a second-rate version. When you make yourself invisible—in business, at home, with your friends, or even with yourself—you always play smaller than your potential.

I spent the majority of my life fighting to find my voice. I waged an internal war and fought with my weight, sexuality, religion, and acceptance from others who would never be able to give me what I needed. I spent years being angry at people for taking my voice away and trying to sequester me into silence. One of my earliest memories of losing my voice was in seventh grade and being sent into the hall to talk with the teacher for what I am sure was obnoxious behavior. Guilty! I don't have any recollection of the conversation, but I do remember him pushing me up against the lockers, the sound echoing down the hall, and feeling embarrassed. It was the first time someone in a position of power had bullied me and used their authority to try and silence me. As a result, I never told anyone about it until now. This incident, along with others, taught me that we never lose our voice. We give it away. We do this when we lose our awareness of its power and find ourselves complicit in the silencing others have projected on us. Sometimes we give up our voice because we are consumed with just trying to survive the relationship, we just want to move on from the immediate situation, or we feel that we don't have the skills to communicate without going full-on *Karate Kid* on the other person. The danger, however, is when you give up your voice, you give up a little bit of your self-worth in the process.

We have all found ourselves in a relationship—whether with a boss, lover, or friend—where we feel like we lose our voice. This often happens when the other person makes the relationship more about themselves and their needs. Instead of standing center stage and speaking up on how their actions are impacting the relationship, we acquiesce until we find ourselves no longer sharing what we feel. Sometimes these individuals weaponize fear to silence you. This often happens when your presence and voice make them question their own identity and they are not ready to look at themselves with that much transparency. They become defensive, and they put their desire to protect their image ahead of their desire to understand you. Be prepared: they will always use shame to keep you silent. This happens every day in society. Someone emotionally or physically abuses their spouse to "keep them in line." A boss or coworker publicly humiliates someone in a meeting as a warning to never do that again. Defense lawyers shame the victims in a case as an attempt to rewrite the narrative the public and jury hears. Companies and organizations issue edicts to coerce employees or players into behaving a certain way. Political leaders cherry-pick facts and then turn social movements into causes they are not, in hopes of galvanizing people to their point of view. Individuals use the internet to bully others. Shaming is nothing more than a coward's way of controlling someone's behavior because they are afraid of what those actions will mean to them.

There is, however, a big difference between being silenced and having the emotional maturity to decide when and how to share your voice so it can best be received. Being silenced will always make you feel like a victim. Choosing the best timing on how you deliver your message is your decision and that is leadership. Sometimes that requires you to be silent in the immediate moment so you can have more of an impact later. Great leaders do not rush to speak. Their silence does not mean disengagement, and they understand their intentional silence can serve a broader purpose. Silence allows leaders to find their wisdom first and the appropriate emotional expression, so they can lovingly speak truth to bullshit and not stand blindly by as someone else distorts the facts as they see them.

> Silence allows leaders to find their wisdom first.

Mark Lagestee, VP of Global Talent and Organization Development at Yum! Brands, taught me an important lesson on being a great leader of yourself and owning your voice. During one of our leadership sessions, he shared a piece of advice that always served him well in his life. That advice was, "what you allow, you encourage." He explained, "How I treat my wife is how my kids will choose to treat their mom. If I allow myself to not help with chores, ignore her when she is talking, or use inappropriate language then my kids will believe they can do the same thing." He went on to explain that what we inevitably allow at work becomes part of the overall culture. If we allow recognition, autonomy, and risk-taking then those elements become important values that shape the entire organization. On the other hand, if you let leaders put results before people, lead out of fear, and undermine the customer experience then you signal to everyone in lower positions that this is what it takes to be successful at this company. Mark's examples are a reminder that your voice is the primary way you establish boundaries in your life. However, when those boundaries are tested, you must own your voice and give yourself permission to stand in both the power of your yes and your no. Do not allow your silence to be taken as permission.

You become complicit in your silencing and give your voice away the moment you:

1. Stop believing your voice means something.

2. Do not honor the voice you already have.

3. Consistently put other's voices above your own.

4. Stop expressing your ideas and feelings.

5. Are more worried about other's reactions than your truth.

6. Do not manage the approach for how you deliver your truth.

HOW ARE YOU GIVING AWAY YOUR VOICE?

1. Review the list of six ways people silence themselves and give their voice away.

2. Identify two out of the six that most contribute to your silencing.

3. All actions serve a purpose, so what purpose are you giving that action in your life?

4. What would be the benefits of changing it?

5. What would you need to do differently so you could make progress in those two identified areas?

Once we accept our responsibility in the chaos we created then we can stand up in it and reclaim our personal power. There will be times in your life when you will be shamed in hopes that you will sequester your feelings and surrender your voice. Refuse to own other people's insecurity. Refuse to go quietly. You will be tested—time and time again—to stand up for who you are. Don't let yourself down.

> You will be tested—time and time again—to stand up for who you are. Don't let yourself down.

EIGHT WAYS TO OWN YOUR AUTHENTIC VOICE

The world was introduced to Susan Boyle on April 11, 2009. She appeared on *Britain's Got Talent* and as she walked to center stage she was met with eye rolls, judgment, and dismissal. Susan had faced many obstacles in her life prior to her audition. She was mocked in school for being different; subsequently, she was diagnosed late in life with Asperger syndrome. By 2009, she had lost her father, sister, and mother. Music was an escape for her. Stepping out to center stage was Susan's opportunity to chase her dream of being a professional singer. When Simon Cowell asked her why it had not worked out so far, Susan responded, "I've never been given the chance before." Her lifetime of preparation and her standout performance left no doubt that a star had arrived.

There are going to be moments in your life when you are standing center stage about to be given an opportunity to make your voice matter, but it is your intentional preparation beforehand that sets you up for success. Roman philosopher Seneca once said, "Luck is what happens when preparation meets opportunity." Susan Boyle's success was a result of years of training and coaching prior to the opportunity of a televised show. Your success will also lie in your ability to be prepared so you, too, can demonstrate that you are a star.

Below are eight communication strategies to help you own your authentic voice and be more prepared when your opportunity presents itself.

MANAGE YOUR LEADERSHIP PRESENCE

According to research from the Center for Talent Innovation, and the 268 senior executives surveyed, your executive presence is based on three foundational factors:

05% – Image (how you look)
28% – Communication (how you speak)
67% – Gravitas (how you act)

All three of these factors impact your ability to own your leadership voice.

Let's talk about why image matters. Five percent might sound like a small number, but it packs a big punch! Image is the first credibility hurdle you must pass professionally. People should not be so distracted by your image that they are not able to hear the message you're trying to communicate. You inevitably hold yourself back when this happens.

The culture of your organization impacts how others view your executive presence and whether your image is appropriate for the environment or not. Always tailor your appearance to the culture. Executive presence does not ask you to compromise who you are. You can be authentic and have a signature style while still fitting in with the organization. As Sylvia Ann Hewlett states in her book, *Executive Presence*, "cracking the appearance code opens doors and puts you in play [. . .] when you make an effort to look polished, you signal to others that you see them as worth your time and investment." Looking good is a matter of perspective and it can be hard for us to be objective about ourselves. Ask for feedback. Don't let your appearance take away from your intellect. You are meant to stand out, but you have a credibility issue when people are talking more about your appearance than your ideas.

Communication comprises 28 percent of your executive presence. I have built an entire career and business on communication skills and what I know for sure is that your success as a communicator lies in your ability to engage your audience. Hand two leaders the exact same material and the one who adds in their personality, stories, and who can empathize with the audience will always be the one who is perceived as more successful and memorable. How you speak is just as important, if not more important, than what you speak about.

"Commander's Intent" is a term used in the military to clearly outline the end goal of any mission on which success will be measured. The end goal focuses on "what" should be accomplished, not "how" it should be done. This gives soldiers under the commander the autonomy to adapt and change course, as needed, so they can achieve the desired intent regardless of what obstacles they face. When it comes to communication, the "commander's intent" is always to engage and connect with your audience. There is no one right way to do that, but it should always be your singular focus when you speak.

Below are the top six communication traits identified from the Center for Talent Innovation's research. Use these traits as guideposts on how you can best engage and connect with your audience:

1. Superior speaking skills.

2. Ability to command a room.

3. Forcefulness and assertiveness.

4. Ability to read a client/boss/room.

5. Sense of humor and ability to banter.

6. Body language/posture.

We live in a world where we are always communicating—whether that is through our words, body language, or digital footprint. It is incumbent on you to ensure how you communicate represents the brand you want to portray. I have been in multiple conversations with leaders when they reference someone's online presence and the negative impact it has on their overall presence and credibility within the workplace. You must have superior speaking skills in person as well as online. I believe your digital voice will shape your legacy long after you are gone. Make sure you are remembered for all the right reasons.

Gravitas is the seriousness and weight of your demeanor, and it constitutes 67 percent of your executive presence. In short, it has to do with how you act as a leader. We all know leaders who are smart, but who lack awareness of how their actions and intensity impact others in the room. It is their lack of gravitas that will prevent them from playing to the level of their potential and being seen as a leader capable of leading in the top levels of the organization.

Gravitas has always reminded me of the word "gravity." Gravity keeps us grounded and it connects us with the center of the earth. Gravitas is not that different. It requires us to stay grounded in our emotional intelligence and connected to our higher self at all times, but especially when things don't go as planned. Famous leaders who display exceptional gravitas when communicating are Barack Obama, Carly Fiorina, Meryl Streep, Arianna Huffington, and Prince William.

Gravitas is emotional intelligence in action.

Gravitas is emotional intelligence in action. It requires leaders to lead with both their head and their heart. People with gravitas are aware of what they feel, but they have the skills and mindset to be able to rise above the intensity of the moment and elevate the conversation in a direct and tactful way. For example, a company I work with had just hired a new president for their business. She had great energy that matched the culture, but she came from a different industry background, so some employees weren't sure what to expect. As an effort to build relationships with others, she hosted a meeting where she talked about who she was and allowed them to ask questions. A prominent and vocal leader in the room raised his hand and asked, "Why should I trust you?" It would have been easy in this moment to become defensive or feel the need to prove yourself by focusing on your past results. However, the president had enough confidence to not take the comment personally and the gravitas to answer in a way that made a connection with everyone in the room. She demonstrated empathy and explained that he had every reason not to trust her right now. She then humbly asked him to trust the people who hired her since he believed in them and to give her the chance to earn his trust. She proved that great leaders, especially in moments of emotionally charged situations, put empathy first and information second. It was her ability to connect and create empathy that allowed her to dampen the intensity in the room while also building her credibility in the process.

The top aspects of gravitas, as identified by leaders in the Center for Talent Innovation's survey, were confidence and grace under fire. Let's explore confidence for a moment. *The Atlantic* published an article in 2014 called, "The Confidence Gap." One of the main questions in the article was, "Is confidence just as important as competence?" The answer is yes. "Success, it turns out, correlates just as closely with confidence as it does with competence." The more confident leaders appeared, the more competent people perceived them as. This is the type of confidence that we refer to as "quiet confidence." It comes from an authentic place where you do not feel you have to prove yourself to anyone. Your words are not rushed, your passion is not distracting, you do not take things personally, and you are comfortable choosing when to own your silence. Anyone can have gravitas when things are going well and everyone is getting along, but the true measure of your gravitas will be tested when you are under pressure and becoming emotionally hijacked. When the shit hits the fan, which it always does at some point, you want to be around a leader who remains calm, emotionally present, and whose energy brings out the best in everyone around them. Be that leader.

TAKE YOUR AUDIENCE WITH YOU

Leaders are always more successful when they can communicate in a way that takes others along with them from the beginning. This often requires us to go slow initially so we can go fast later. Sometimes, in our desire to prove our point, we fail to take others with us. We hit them upside the head with our facts, opinions, and beliefs and then expect them to agree with us. The reality is, they often don't. Our lack of transparency around why we believe what we do and our inability to align the conversation with what we agree on only drives deeper disconnection and distrust among others with a different perspective.

There are two effective and widely-known techniques on how you can create buy-in from the beginning of any message you deliver. One of them is from Dale Carnegie and the other is from Alan H. Monroe.

Dale Carnegie, in his best-selling book *How to Win Friends and Influence People*, shares a technique called "Yes, Yes." The idea is that you communicate and emphasize what you and your audience agree on versus focusing on what you disagree on. The goal is that your audience feels like you get them and they psychologically say, "Yes, that's exactly what I feel . . . Yes, I've been there . . . Yes, you get what I'm going through." I start many of my keynote presentations with this technique. For example, I might say, "I want you to say 'yes' if you feel like sometimes you get so busy being busy that you lose yourself in the process. Yes? And say 'yes' if you believe that to be a great leader of other people you must be willing to slow down and be a great leader of yourself, first. Yes?" The entire audience always yells, "yes" and, more importantly, I have set the context for what we are going to discuss and already received their buy-in to the core message. You can do something very similar in a one-on-one conversation when you want to validate someone's experience. For example, "Wow. It sounds like you're really frustrated because you worked over 60 hours last week and had to sacrifice your family time and all you want is to be appreciated and acknowledged by your manager." If you have really gotten to the heart of what that person is trying to describe then they will either nod their head in agreement or verbally acknowledge what you said. Your ability to build trust and connection with other people is cultivated in moments of yes.

Clinical psychiatrist Alan H. Monroe created a persuasive argument technique that has been around since the 1930s and is now commonly referred to as Monroe's Motivated Sequence. The formula builds on the key elements people often need to satisfy in their minds before they are willing to act. As a result of its effectiveness, it has been taught to politicians, salespeople, and leaders for decades. I have found a lot of success using this model when making my pitch to a potential client, reframing a conversation in a meeting, helping a sales team outline their messaging for their next finalist meeting, and providing an awesome closing summary to my presentations. The formula consists of five key steps:

Step 1: Grab Their Attention
This step calls your audience to attention and gets them interested in what you have to say.

Step 2: Frame the Need
This step is the key to taking people with you when communicating because it fundamentally requires you to get outside of your perspective and step into the listener's mind so you can anchor your solution to their specific needs, wants, and/or concerns. It is here where the listener says, "Yes, you're right!" This is an excellent place to create a sense of urgency around the need and then provide specific evidence and examples to support your claim.

Step 3: Satisfy the Need
This is where you propose your solution and show your audience how it will work.

Step 4: Visualize the Future
This is where you offer people a bold promise for what the future could look like if the solution were implemented and/or you articulate the consequences of not implementing the solution.

Step 5: Call to Action
This is where you provide your audience with a specific step on how they can be a part of that bold promise and you invite them to join you. Make the action step easy to understand and something they can immediately do.

EXAMPLE:
1. We know from research that emotional intelligence is more of a predictor of success than IQ.

2. If you are like every other leadership team I've worked with then you have leaders in your organization who you know are capable of playing bigger, but who just can't seem to get out of their own way. Their ego gets

the best of them, they put results before people, and their intensity erodes their character and credibility.

3. As an executive coach, my job is to come in and create a safe space where I can turn the mirror on these leaders and get them to tell the truth about how they show up, take accountability for the energy they use to get results, and help them cultivate stronger emotional intelligence. I do that by working with each leader for a period of six months. During that time, the leader takes a pre- and post-emotional intelligence 360 assessment, engages in both face-to-face and virtual coaching sessions, and intentionally builds targeted relationships with stakeholders in the organization.

4. Everyone in the organization wins when leaders take the time to grow their emotional intelligence. Specifically, leaders learn how to lead with both their head and heart, engagement on teams increases, and you build a culture that realizes how you get results is just as important as the results themselves.

5. I would love to leave you some more detailed information about what this would look like in your organization and then connect next week on how we can make this happen and answer any more of your questions. When would be a good day for you to meet?

Be brief
and be brilliant.

Great leaders communicate in a way that moves the conversation forward. They do not talk to just hear themselves talk or to validate their own ego. Monroe's Motivated Sequence challenges you to consider your own thinking and it gives you a clear process on how you can be brief and be brilliant. Each step is intentionally building your ability to take other people with you, so do not feel like you have to go through every step before engaging in a conversation with your audience.

Have you ever found yourself in a meeting where it feels like everyone is talking in circles and the conversation is not moving forward in a productive way? Be the type of leader who can rise above the intensity in the moment and whose words can get everyone back on the boat and rowing in the same direction. You can use Monroe's Motivated Sequence to reframe any conversation. You do that by refocusing and getting people bought into the overall problem, concern, or need.

You already have a powerful voice, so just continue finding techniques that allow you to maximize its effectiveness. Dale Carnegie and Alan H. Monroe's techniques are two great places for you to start.

USE YOUR BODY LANGUAGE TO DEMONSTRATE CONFIDENCE

Body language is a sexy topic that fascinates most people, and everyone wants to learn how to see what so many other people miss. However, when you become fixated on analyzing other people's body language you stop listening and you stop holding the space for connection. Quit worrying about everyone else's body language. You cannot control what is going on in their minds or how they choose to show up. What you can control is how your presence is communicating the message you want and if your presence is inviting connection.

I spent years studying nonverbal communication and I received certification in body language from The Body Language Institute where I was taught by Janine Driver, former FBI agent and author of the *New York Times* bestseller *You Say More Than You Think*. I fundamentally believe that our body language is just a manifestation of our conscious and subconscious thoughts and feelings, and it is one of the most important elements when it comes to building trust and connection with others. I cannot make you a body language expert, nor do you need to be. I cannot teach you everything you need to know when it comes to understanding how context, consistency, congruence, clusters, culture, and gender differences impact body language. What I can do is provide you with some basic principles that will help you to take accountability for your presence and use your body language to connect better with others.

So, here is rule #1: body language is about perception, not what you want it to mean. Your job is to manage that perception to the extent that you can control it. I have coached individuals who would look at me after I taught some of these body language concepts and say, "I am never going to do that," or "That's not what I meant when I did that." To be frank, I am not here to shame you, change you, or convince you to show up differently. How you show up is your choice and I will respect whatever decision you make. However, I owe it to you to provide the information you say you want so you can align your body language with the best version of yourself.

> Body language is about perception, not what you want it to mean.

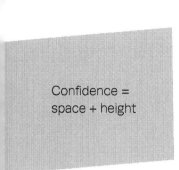

Confidence =
space + height

The best place to start is with confidence. The formula I teach people in my workshops is that confidence = space + height. You will be perceived as more confident by the appropriate amount of space you take up and the height you have. All my vertically challenged friends typically get nervous when I share that formula, but relax. Confidence is not about being the tallest person in the room. It is about owning the space and height you are able to own. If you want to learn how to take up more space and height then channel your inner Beyoncé. She has mastered the art and science of projecting confidence and looking like a badass.

There are four power zones on the body that, if you keep open and use them appropriately, will help you take up more space and height so you can be perceived as confident. They are your neck dimple, torso, naughty bits, and feet.

Your first power zone is your neck dimple. You probably didn't even know you have a neck dimple! This is that small indentation right under your throat area and above your collar bones. Many leaders are taught when speaking to keep their neck open and head forward. The moment you put your hand over your neck dimple (to rub your neck, adjust your tie, play with your jewelry) you do not appear as confident or comfortable. I assume Tyra Banks never went through body language training, but she has taken and scrutinized enough pictures to know what confidence and power look like. She always told the girls on America's Next Top Model to, "elongate your neck." So, if you don't believe me, believe a supermodel who has used her skills, knowledge, and confidence to become a multimillionaire.

The second power zone is your torso. Think of this zone as your superhero logo on display for the world! Watch what happens when you get in an elevator with a bunch of people you don't know. If you have something in your hands you will, more than likely, take them and cover up your torso area. Why? If you are like me then you grew up constantly being warned of "Stranger Danger." When your subconscious mind is not comfortable, you take what you have control over to protect yourself. In this case, you are able to use your arms and materials in your hands to shield yourself and protect the vulnerable organs in your body. Watch contestants on reality television when they are about to be eliminated. Many of them will cross one arm over their torso area and grab their opposite wrist or arm. This gesture does not look nearly as confident as when you keep this power zone open.

The third power zone is your naughty bits. Yes, you really did just read that correctly! "Naughty bits" is how I learned it and it is the most politically correct word choice I could use out of all the options available, so I am going with it. Think about how most men sit in a chair when they are comfortable. They generally plop down, take up a lot of space, and open their legs like Al Bundy, from *Married with Children*, sitting on his couch. Men typically do not sit like this if they are not comfortable. Granted, this gesture can be perceived as overconfident and too comfortable, so it is important that leaders be mindful of their surroundings. I have seen both men and women get up to present and stand with their hands covering up their naughty bits in what is traditionally known as the "fig leaf" hand position. We do not have to create a story about why they are standing that way. The reality is they do not appear as confident as someone who gets up and is able to keep their power zones open and use appropriate gestures to enhance their message. One final note on the bits! Pay attention this week to actors, billboards, magazines, and people in the office. Watch how many times you see someone put their hands in their pockets while hooking their thumbs on the outside. This gesture always comes across as casual confidence. You have probably never thought about it before, but do you know why? What that person is subconsciously doing is pointing a big arrow right to their naughty bits and you would never do that if you were nervous and uncomfortable. So, here is my final piece of advice when it comes to using this particular power zone to project confidence: when in doubt, frame the bits!

> When in doubt, frame the bits!

The final power zone is your feet. Who would you perceive as more confident between the following two speakers? The speaker who is standing with their feet shoulder width apart and who uses their gestures to enhance what they are saying or the speaker who stands with their feet together? You will always recognize the person who keeps the power zones open as more confident and comfortable.

USE YOUR BODY LANGUAGE TO DEMONSTRATE EMPATHY

Brené Brown once defined empathy as, "feeling with people." These are the important moments where we don't need to show up as confident and powerful in our conversations. Those individuals need us to be inclusive and vulnerably present. This requires us to flex our style so we can show up in a way that best serves and builds trust in the relationship. To do that, I typically break all the rules I shared with you on the body language of confidence. Remember: there is a time to be powerful and confident, but then there is a time to be collaborative and empathetic. That posturing looks and feels different. Sylvia Ann Hewlett says, "to radiate presence you have to radiate that you are present." Below are four body language gestures that will support your ability to be perceived as present and empathetic for others.

Feet

Your feet are the most honest part of your body and will face the direction of your intention and interest. The energy between you and the other person feels completely different when you look at them with your face/eyes but keep your feet pointed in a different direction. Therefore, show up for people by ensuring you point your feet towards them when communicating. It impacts the dynamic of the conversation.

Eye Contact

Eye contact is one of the most important ways we demonstrate that we are showing up for someone. How much eye contact do you think you should consistently maintain with someone during a one-on-one conversation? I always have someone yell, "100 percent" in the workshops I teach. No! Stop it. It's creepy and no one likes it. The reality is that the amount of eye contact changes based on the situation and whether you are listening or talking; however, a good rule of thumb is that you should maintain between 60-70 percent consistent eye contact if you want to create an emotional connection. Anything above 80 percent consistent eye contact is often seen as intimidation. You must be so present that you know how to use your eye contact to create space in the conversation and give people a break when they need it.

Lean In

Space plays an important role in our ability to be perceived as interested. In general, we get closer to things we like and we create distance between us and the things we don't like. Therefore, when we lean into a conversation the perception is that we are interested. Now, don't take it too far. Give people their space and if you notice them leaning away or backing up then take a hint!

Head Tilt and Slow Nod
The head tilt and nod is one of the most notable gender differences in body language. Men typically keep their head straight forward and only nod when they agree. Women, on the other hand, typically tilt their head and nod slowly as a signal that they are listening. Tilting and nodding is a highly empathetic gesture to say, "I get you. I hear you. Tell me more about that." However, be aware when anyone starts to nod their head rapidly during the conversation. They are usually signaling that you should speed it up!

My pastor, David Emery, once said, "You cannot meet people where they are when you think you are above them." Great leaders have both the awareness and the willingness to flex their style so they can connect better with others. In their ability to flex they find the true power of their voice.

LISTEN BELOW THE WATERLINE

I was riding in the car with a client as we made our way to the next workshop I was teaching. I found myself growing frustrated and concerned throughout the ride because this woman leader seemed to be so judgmental and negative about most things in life. I held my tongue because I wasn't sure if I had earned the right to say anything based on our current relationship. The more I listened, the more I felt like there was some story or feeling underneath everything she was saying that she was not sharing. Finally, on the way home, I made the choice to say something—regardless of whether it cost me the relationship with her and any future income. I said, "Can I ask you a question?" After she gave me permission I directly said, "Do you think you might be overly critical of yourself and everyone else in life?" Silence. I explained to her that we often see in other people what we refuse to see in ourselves. The rest of the ride home was uncomfortable and transactional at best. I remember leaving her car thinking, "Well, that just happened! Been nice knowing you." I received an email two weeks later where she thanked me. She said the question triggered a lot inside her. Her initial reaction was, "Fuck you! How dare you." She indicated that she was expecting everyone else around her to change when the truth is she was avoiding looking at herself. She disclosed that she was addicted to Adderall and she was dying on the inside. She needed help. As a result, she was admitting herself into rehab. This woman came out of rehab refreshed, with a new perspective, and said, "I have no more secrets. I feel liberated." Today, she is successful in her leadership roles, a supportive and unconditionally loving mother, and a certified crisis coach helping people with their transformations in life.

Your ability to be a great leader will never trump your ability to be a great listener. You can listen to be right or listen to understand, but you cannot do both. Each of those requires a different intention and presence in the conversation. Leaders who do not listen or who only listen to be right take more than just your time and energy; they take your trust. Listening to understand requires intentionality and for you to listen deeper than just the words being said. Thich Nhat Hanh, Vietnamese Buddhist monk and peace activist, describes deep listening as, "the kind of listening that can relieve the suffering of the other person. You listen with one purpose: help him or her to empty his heart."

> You can listen to be right or listen to understand, but you cannot do both.

There are three different levels of listening you should know if you want to own your voice and communicate with stronger impact. Your ability to identify which level you are showing up in gives you the clarity you need to connect and lead better.

Level 1: Ego Listening
Focus: Me
Intent: Listen to be right
Core Actions: Thinking about how to respond, thinking how the information applies to you, not fully present, critical of the information, constantly interrupting

Level 2: Active Listening
Focus: You
Intent: Listen to understand what is being said
Core Actions: Listening to the words, leaning forward, tilting/nodding head when appropriate, feet facing the individual, paraphrasing, asking follow-up questions

Level 3: Deep Listening
Focus: Energy

Intent: Listen to understand what is not being said

Core Actions: Identifying the emotion underneath someone's words, being aware of and adapting to body language, acknowledging and validating someone's feelings, trusting your intuition and seeking clarity on what's not being directly said

The strategy I teach leaders on how to listen and communicate more effectively is to "listen below the waterline"—which is level 3, deep listening. Many of us have learned from science class that around 90 percent of an iceberg is under water, thus leaving only ten percent visible on the surface. That ten percent is what many of us base our observations and judgments on. However, there is so much more depth and context to just what our eyes can see. I believe how we communicate is similar. The actual words people use to impart their point of view only make up a small percentage of what you really need to hear in any given conversation. Their words are the visible part of the iceberg. Underneath their words are all these other elements that, if we can slow down long enough and tune into what they are, will help us navigate every conversation and relationship more effectively. Tuning in requires us to listen to what is not being directly said and to be aware of a shift of energy. That shift of energy comes in the form of body language, tone, and emotions. Being able to listen for those shifts often allows us to go underneath the waterline and address what is not being said like intent, beliefs, interpretations, and assumptions.

Being a great listener is not about fixing people or feeling the need to share your perspective. It is about recognizing where you are in the moment and how your presence is impacting the other person. Without understanding the three levels of listening then you cannot own the power of your voice. Sometimes the most effective choice you can make as a leader is to talk less and listen more. How you listen is just as important as your ability to listen.

> How you listen is just as important as your ability to listen.

ASK BETTER QUESTIONS

All questions are not created equal. Close-ended questions skim the surface and have a yes or no answer. They often bring the conversation to a halt and do not challenge people to higher levels of thinking. An example would be asking,

All questions are not created equal.

"Did you do that?" Open-ended questions cannot be answered with a simple yes or no response. They force the responder to elaborate, but they do not necessarily move them forward. For example, I had a woman disclose to me that she committed an act of violence in self-defense. Asking her, "What did you do?" might satisfy my selfish curiosity, but it does not serve her and her healing. Questions like this only keep individuals stuck in the drama of their story. Therefore, our goal is to ask open-ended questions that urge the client to look at the core issue, often addressing what's not being said, so they can make choices and move forward with accountability. When the quality of our questions sparks someone to create new insight for themselves then they start the process of climbing out of their drama. These are what I refer to as empowering questions. When that woman came to me and talked about being abused and how she wanted to move forward with her life I asked, "So, what do you need to forgive yourself for?" I could have asked, "What thoughts do you need to let go of so you can show up as your best self now?" or, "How do you get back to that confident woman who allows herself to be loved again?" Empowering questions aren't as worried about what happened in the past. They target what you are emotionally experiencing today and help you drive forward momentum.

These types of questions are just as powerful in a work context. One of the best leaders I have seen be able to ask empowering questions that challenge a team to do bigger and bolder things is Kathy Gosser, Director of Learning and Organizational Development at the KFC Corporation. She has a gift for being able to pull the right people together in a room and ask questions like, "What would it take for us to provide an exceptional learning experience for our franchise partners?" or "What would it look like if it did work?" Her questions always take people where they are and challenge them to think bigger. For example, when Kathy started studying the value of microlearning she brought her training team together and asked, "How could this look at KFC?" That single question both activated her team's curiosity and gave them the space to imagine what the future could be. They have now launched an entire "Learning Nuggets" platform with over 200 bite-size modules in a variety of topics. This concept provided so much relevance and value to the business that now the team is constantly in meetings where internal and external partners say, "We need a nugget on that!" Kathy's leadership style proves that your value as a leader is not in having all the answers or even in asking a bunch of questions that do not spark insight. Your value is in the quality of questions you ask. Therefore, ask empowering questions and then give people the space to be brilliant.

Finally, sometimes before you ask better questions you need to be transparent with your intention for asking them. You can identify your real motive by answering this question: what do I hope to gain from asking this? Opening up your question with clarity as to why you are asking it creates trust and makes people less skeptical about your intent.

I had a client who received his emotional intelligence 360 feedback. He questioned one of the scores from his manager and was going to ask him, "Can you help me understand why you gave me that result?" This close-ended question can come across as too direct and defensive, even with the appropriate tone. He and I talked about the importance of sometimes laying the framework for why we are asking questions—especially when a conversation has the possibility to turn into a difficult one. His intention for asking the question was so he could understand his manager's perspective and use it to aid in his future development. Therefore, his approach to his manager might sound something like this: "You know moving up in the organization is my long-term goal, so I've been reflecting a lot on my 360 feedback. I want to be able to use the data to learn as much as I can, make necessary adjustments, and move forward as effectively as possible. I noticed my score on one question was different from everyone else's and I think it would be valuable for me to understand your point of view. What is your perspective on this issue and what would success look like to you if I was doing it well?" This approach sounds completely different and fosters collaboration.

SHOW YOUR PERSONALITY
Norma Bates, in the hit television show *Bates Motel*, was preparing a presentation she had to deliver, and the advice she received is a good lesson for all of us: "Don't be so worried about the information that you leave yourself at home. You're the best part."

Competence alone is not enough to connect. When leaders rely only on their competence to deliver their message, they become rigid and often get caught up in trying to prove why their thoughts or ideas are the "right" ones. The focus becomes only on getting through their slides or their talking points and they miss small meaningful moments to connect and build trust with their audience. Authors Kouzes and Posner have spent their careers studying what makes a leader credible, and the top four traits of admired leaders are that they are 1) honest, 2) forward-looking, 3) inspiring, and 4) competent. Competence matters, but when that is all you rely on you fail to inspire others and you make it harder for your audience to buy into the big picture of where you are trying to lead them.

If your energy and personality do not add to the effectiveness of your message then you have made yourself into a commodity that can be easily replaced. You are better than that! You are meant to shine, but standing in the sunshine requires you to step completely into the light. You cannot fully shine when you leave part of yourself in the dark.

Great leaders understand that people buy into them before they ever buy into their message. They accept that authenticity and vulnerability are what it takes to connect and humanize themselves to others. One of the easiest ways to do that is through stories. The reality is facts don't change people, stories change people. Therefore, great leaders utilize stories to bring their facts to life. Your personality is not one-dimensional and you owe it to yourself to share all sides of it. Stories allow you to show the funny, sad, quirky, successful, and could-only-happen-to-me dimensions of who you are. Get rid of the antiquated notion that you have to hide part of who you are to be noticed, to be accepted, and to be successful. The tribe that is worth your time and attention needs and loves all sides of you.

USE YOUR VOICE TO STAND FOR SOMETHING

One of the most radical ways to change how you perceive the power of your voice is by understanding what your voice stands for based on the people that came before you. In a world where so many people only yell about what they are against, it is important that you change the narrative and use your voice to stand for something. Standing for something elevates the conversation and keeps you connected to your moral compass. Additionally, it empowers you to bring with you the collective energy of the people you represent when you speak. When that happens, you realize you are never alone and that your voice is a change agent in this world.

You can discover what you stand for when you map out the critical people in your life (past or present), the experiences they endured, and how you can use your voice to either stand up or atone for them. For example, my mother's dream was to be a nurse. She gave up that dream because she did not have the financial resources to pursue it when she was younger. I now get to be a voice for every woman who feels like they did not get to live up to their potential or who did not know how to go after what they wanted. I have ancestors that moved from England to the United States in the 1600s. I imagine the risk and fear it took to sacrifice everything for the potential of a better life. For that, I use my voice to empower people to live a bold life. I also use my voice for both the moral achievements and atonement of my ancestors. I use my voice for every person who has felt different and had to struggle with their identity and sense of self-worth. And I use my voice to stand for everything that does not directly impact me because of my privilege. I am never alone when I speak, and I fully accept that my voice is so much bigger than just me.

I AM A VOICE FOR . . .

1. Map out 10 people (past or present) who you believe have significantly shaped your voice.

2. Next to their names, write out some of the critical experiences in their life.

3. Next to their experiences, write out how you can use your voice to stand up or atone for them.

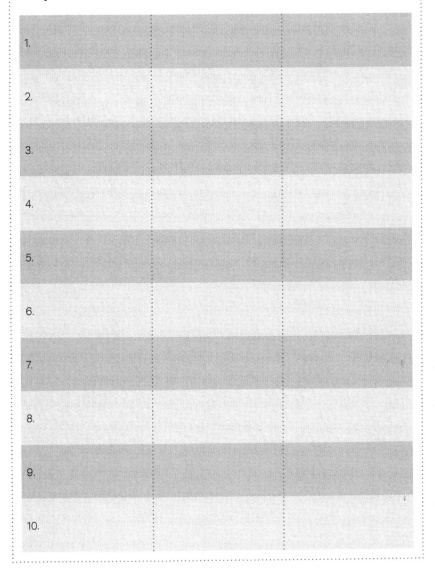

1.

2.

3.

4.

5.

6.

7.

8.

9.

10.

4. Once your entire list is done, write 3-5 statements starting with, "I am a voice for . . . "

5. How does this exercise alter the way you see your voice?

Your voice was shaped by all the people before you, but I believe your voice and presence will also shape every generation that follows your legacy. You make a choice every day to use your voice to bend the arc of humanity, either towards progress for all or back to the privilege of a select few. There are millions of people who need you to speak up and be their voice in a world where they feel unheard, unseen, and undervalued. Your voice is a representation of what you believe. Please never excuse yourself out of your own greatness. Offer yourself more by speaking up in ways that are meaningful to you. You are standing on the shoulders of generations, and with that you carry their dreams, their challenges, their successes, and their perspective. Accept this gift graciously and use it with purpose and intention.

FINAL THOUGHT ON STANDING CENTER STAGE AND OWNING YOUR VOICE

In Marianne Williamson's best-selling novel, *A Return to Love*—the book that fundamentally shifted my perspective on life—she says, "Your playing small does not serve the world. There is nothing enlightened about shrinking so that others do not feel insecure around you [. . .] As we let our own light shine, we unconsciously give other people permission to do the same. As we're liberated from our own fear, our presence automatically liberates others."

Standing in your light and owning your voice is an uncomfortable and vulnerable process. You are giving yourself permission to stand center stage and with that choice you are inviting the world to see, experience, and even critique what you offer. Standing center stage does not require permission or approval from other people. It requires you to believe that what you say means something and you owe it to yourself and to others to use the platform you've been given to share your voice and presence unapologetically. It is accepting the rewards and consequences that come from standing center stage and trusting that you will learn the lessons you need to learn to continue to move forward in your journey.

> Standing center stage does not require permission or approval from other people.

Standing center stage won't always be easy, but one day you will wake up and realize it is where you've always belonged. Center stage is where you found your voice, and center stage is where you made your voice and presence matter. Please trust that this world needs your voice in the way only you can speak it and share it. Your voice is the key to your liberation and the window for someone else's.

COMMITMENT EXERCISE

What are you willing to commit to doing differently this next week so you can practice some of the skills provided and own your authentic voice?

AFFIRMATION

Today, I will step out from behind the shadows I feel comfortable in, and allow myself to stand center stage in my own life. Standing center stage might not feel comfortable, but I acknowledge that I am worth that choice; therefore, I stand there—not in a braggadocian or egotistical way—but in a way where I can illuminate the truth of who I am and who I have always been. Standing center stage requires me to speak up and own the voice I have been gifted, so today I will share my thoughts and ideas, ask for what I want, and express myself without the fear of judgment. I feel empowered and confident every time I own my voice, so I use these moments as a gentle reminder as to why I must keep speaking up. I own my voice today for everyone who has believed in me. I own my voice today for everyone who needs to hear my message and story in the way only I can share it. And I own my voice today for myself, so I can look back on my life and say, "I was here. I spoke up. I made my presence matter."

CHAPTER FIVE
LEADERSHIP SUMMARY

- A champion is an individual with the relentless determination to rise up—again and again—in order to better themselves and others.

- Champions are not the result of luck or chance. They are defined by three core actions: a mindset of relentless determination, a focus on achievement over winning, and the ability to stand up for both themselves and others.

- All champions are leaders, but not all leaders are champions.

- If you want to play bigger in your life then start acting like a champion.

5

want to be a great leader of yourself?

ACT LIKE A CHAMPION

A champion is
A person who rises up –
Again and again.

My definition of what it means to be a champion has evolved throughout my life. As a little boy, I saw a champion as some fictional character with superhero abilities. My innocent mind admired and wanted to be like He-Man who was always saving the world from the evil Skeletor. I had all the fictional characters and their castles, and I would often stand in my living room holding up my imaginary sword screaming, "I have the power." *Clearly, I didn't—so I found myself back in first grade with Ms. McIntosh.*

As a teenager, my definition of what it meant to be a champion evolved into real people with superhuman abilities like police officers, firefighters, and Olympic athletes such as gymnast Kerri Strug and diver Greg Louganis. I will never forget the anxiety, anticipation, and deep respect I felt as both Strug and Louganis stepped up in the face of physical obstacles to pursue their goal and represent something bigger than themselves. These individuals demonstrated a ferocious amount of courage and perseverance. I didn't associate everyday people with having these characteristics, so I admired them for it.

As an adult, I do my best to cherish the good times because I have seen and experienced how life can sucker punch us at any unexpected moment. People that we love die, people get cancer and other diseases, people's lives are uprooted due to violence and war, people face what appears to be insurmountable financial struggle, and people's relationships and careers fall apart. All these experiences have taught me one profound lesson: we don't find ourselves on top of the mountain. We discover our strength and resilience on the journey to the top. The summit is just the reward for not giving up on ourselves.

> We don't find ourselves on top of the mountain.

In 1998, my mom had to endure the loss of her father, the loss of her husband, figure out a way to deal with her own grief while helping her two children deal with theirs, decide how to take care of an 11 1/2 acre farm in Kentucky, and grapple with being a single parent and the financial pressures that come with that. The journey was not easy and I cannot pretend to understand the emotional turmoil she experienced. What I do know, however, is she did not give up on herself and she did not give up on us. She found the will to pick herself up—even on days she did not feel like it. Her actions taught me what it means to be an everyday champion in life, and I believe that is one of the greatest gifts she could have given me.

ACT LIKE A CHAMPION

1. In your own words, define what it means to be a champion.

2. What experiences have shaped your definition of that word?

3. How are you doing at living that word out in your life?

4. If needed, redefine the word in a way that supports your self-concept and self-confidence.

HOW 200 LEADERS DEFINE THE WORD "CHAMPION"

I ask participants in my workshops to close their eyes and think of a leader they admire. They recall how this individual communicates, interacts, motivates, and coaches differently from other leaders. Afterwards, participants open their eyes and share the actions that made them so effective. As you listen to participants talk about this admired leader, that leader's actions move past a transactional employee-employer relationship to someone who had a transformational impact on their life. The language they use when talking about this leader is like that of a champion. So, I became curious. How do leaders across the country define the word "champion" and what does it take to be a champion for others?

I launched a nationwide survey with over 200 leaders from all different age groups and industries. I wanted to know how leaders defined the word "champion" and how our ability to be a champion impacts how we lead and communicate.

Perhaps the most notable finding was the way leaders defined a champion made it achievable for everyone. This title is not just reserved for an elite few with superhuman abilities or accomplishments, like I had defined it as a teenager. It is about everyday people, just like you and me, using their voice and presence—right where they are—to make a positive mark on the world. After analyzing the results of all 200 leaders surveyed, here is how they defined a champion:

A champion is an individual with the relentless determination to rise up—*again and again*—in order to better themselves and others.

ACT LIKE A CHAMPION

A LEADER YOU ADMIRE

1. Think about a leader you really admire (someone you've worked for or someone famous).

2. What do they do differently from other leaders that makes them stand out?

3. Write down 3-4 of the most important actions that contributed to you seeing them as a champion.

4. What is a common theme between all or most of the actions you listed?

5. What does that reinforce or teach you about leadership in general?

6. What does it teach you about your own leadership and communication style?

THREE DEFINING BEHAVIORS ON HOW CHAMPIONS ACT

This research with over 200 leaders not only provided a clear, consistent pattern in how people defined a champion, but they also identified specific behaviors champions demonstrate to be perceived that way. Three core themes emerged that helped shape the definition of what it means to be a champion, and they all connect back to a leader's credibility. Those three themes are:

1. Champions own a mindset of relentless determination.
2. Champions focus on achievement over winning.
3. Champions stand up for both themselves and others.

CHAMPIONS OWN A MINDSET OF RELENTLESS DETERMINATION

There are single moms and single dads who rise up every day with the relentless determination to provide for their kids—even when this is hard and often exhausting. They overcome setbacks and they do what they have to do to put food on the table, create a safe environment, and offer their kids a better life than they had. It is their undefeatable spirit that leaves a mark on their children and why so many survey responders listed their parents as the champions in their lives. They used phrases like, "goes above and beyond", "overcomes challenges", "never gives up", and "persistent" to describe their champion. It proves that being a champion is a mindset followed by intentional action.

> Being a champion is a mindset followed by intentional action.

My best friend Jenna called me up one day during the process of writing this book and said, "You know what I have always admired about you? You have always been a doer and not a talker, but you have been doing a lot of talking about your book." She was right. I was passionate about writing my book, but my passion was not translating into action. I learned that transformation happens through intentional daily commitment, not passion. Plenty of people are passionate about accomplishing their goals, but this does not lead to action. As a result, they never write their book, never get their degree, never apply for the job they want, don't build the relationships that would lead to more opportunities, or they don't become a thought leader in their field. Passion can make us sound big when we are playing small. Passion has you dream of the future while standing in cement. Relentless determination is all about taking bold actions and moving forward.

Pulling yourself out of your current situation and moving forward requires you to create a cadence of how you accomplish the things you say you want to achieve. The reason champions play bigger than others is because they train bigger. They create an intentional routine that they hold themselves accountable to, even on the days they do not feel like it and, as a result, they get better. Athletes aren't motivated to get up every morning and work out, but they do it anyway because that's what the best athletes do. Authors aren't always inspired to write, but they sit down and write anyway because that's what the best authors do. Leaders don't always have the time or energy to build relationships in the workplace, but they do it anyway because that's what the best leaders do. It is your ability to create a cadence in your life that will set you up for more success and cause others to respect you.

Author Simon Sinek says, "Champions are not the ones who always win races—champions are the ones who get out there and try. And try harder the next time. And even harder the next time. Champion is a state of mind. They are devoted. They compete to best themselves as much if not more than they compete to best others." A champion's success is cultivated from a lifetime of persistence, lessons rooted in the agony of pain and short-term failure, and the ability to never stop moving towards their vision. Sometimes champions take those steps with courage and tenacity, and other times they take them with fear. Regardless, they have the courage and willingness to take the steps anyway.

Relentless determination is your declaration to the world that you might not know where you are going, but you are not staying where you are.

CREATING A CADENCE IN YOUR LIFE

1. Identify one or two goals you want to complete this year (personal and/or professional).

2. What is the minimum consistent routine(s) you would hold yourself accountable to if you were serious about achieving those goals?

3. What is the maximum consistent routine(s) you would hold yourself accountable to if you were serious about achieving those goals?

4. Identify two people you trust to hold you accountable and be your cheerleader on your cadence.

5. What is the best way they can support you along your journey?

CHAMPIONS FOCUS ON ACHIEVEMENT OVER WINNING

Survey responders made a distinction between winning and achievement. They defined winning as being focused solely on the destination or the final outcome. There have been plenty of people in history who "won" at the cost of others and who had no regard for how their actions impacted them. These leaders show up with an "I win, you lose" mentality and they manipulate, use, or bully others to get to their end goal. Many of these individuals will bail out of their goals when they don't work or find solace in becoming the victim and blaming others.

Achievement, however, is about the journey and being focused on the effort it takes to accomplish goals. There will be times you get knocked down and face unexpected obstacles that prevent you from reaching your target. Champions, of course, get disappointed, frustrated, and even angry during these moments. Working towards a goal is a very personal and emotional experience when you are showing up and giving all of yourself. However, champions don't wallow in their perceived short-term failure. They learn from it, pick themselves back up, and realign their actions based on what they learned.

Diana Nyad is someone I consider a champion and who teaches us an important lesson on the difference between achievement versus winning. She is a long-distance swimmer who, in 2013 at the age of 64 and on her fifth attempt, swam from Cuba to Key West, Florida without the use of a shark cage. Her successful swim, which she contributes to being part of such a great team, took just under 53 hours and covered a distance of more than 100 miles. Diana started in pursuit of this goal in 1978 when she was 28. In her four previous attempts, over the course of 30 years, obstacles like weather, water temperatures, and jellyfish stings caused her to stop short of accomplishing her ambition. However, she never gave up on herself, her team, and her goal. Diana states in her 2013 TED talk that her mantra in training became, "Find a way!" And isn't that what champions do? They understand that there is no one "right" way and finding a way doesn't mean you are always going to accomplish your goal on your first attempt or in the time frame that you expect. What it means is that you get a vision, take intentional steps to accomplish that vision, and you do it with integrity.

Responders were clear that you can be a winner while not being a champion, and champions don't always have to end up in first place to earn that title.

People who become champions give themselves radical permission to go for a cause they believe in, screw it up, pick themselves up, and go again. They have been shaped by their failures and their character was cultivated in the trenches of life's challenges. They accept that it is not the final result that defines who they are, but how they show up and respond along the journey.

I've had the opportunity to hike at the beautiful Pololū Valley on the Big Island of Hawaii several times and it has taught me an important lesson on leadership. We are all able to show up our best when things are going well and the journey is easy, but what matters is how we show up when the journey gets difficult and we are still driving so hard to accomplish our goals. The trek up the mountain is never easy. We often put our head down and step rock-over-rock in pursuit of the end result. Sometimes, in an effort to make it to the top quickly, we get so far ahead of the people we are with that we leave them behind. We fail to meet them where they are. We fail to take them with us. We fail to look out for the people who mean the most to us. We fail to enjoy the present moment. We communicate with intensity rather than compassion. We do this in both our personal relationships and our jobs. In the end, it doesn't matter if you make it to the top first if you are the only one standing there. Champions understand the journey is just as important as the destination. The destination might be an indication of your success, but the journey is a testament to your character.

Character is the key ingredient in what it takes to be a champion and it is at the core of what it means to put achievement over winning. *The Royal Path of Life* written by T. L. Haines & L. W. Yaggy states that the strength of one's character is based on two things: power of will and power of self-restraint. They go on to say, "You must measure the strength of people by the power of feelings they subdue, not by the power of those feelings which subdue them. Hence, composure is very often the highest resolve of strength." Behaviors that erode someone's character and prevent them from being a champion for others come in the form of lying, stealing, bullying, unwillingness to follow standard rules and processes, refusal to take accountability, or apathy—to name a few. People with these traits lack the self-awareness and/or the self-restraint to manage their behavior and, as a result, they erode their credibility to a point where others are no longer willing to tolerate it. Think of famous people who have been the best in their field with regards to competence, but who ruined their career because they were not as intentional with managing their character. Names like Tiger Woods, Michael Vick, Lindsay Lohan,

Ryan Lochte, Roseanne Barr, Bill Cosby, Paula Deen, and Lance Armstrong always come up. What it proves is that how you act is just as important to your leadership impact, and I would argue even more important, than what you know and what you win. You can be relentless in pursuit of your goals without sacrificing your character in the process.

ONLY FOCUSED ON THE DESTINATION

1. Recall a time you got so caught up in the destination that you forgot to enjoy the journey (i.e., vacation trip, work project, winning someone's affection, presentation, family function).

2. How did you show up when you were only focused on the end result?

3. What did that cost you?

4. How could you have approached it differently?

5. How can you carry those lessons forward?

CHAMPIONS STAND UP FOR BOTH THEMSELVES AND OTHERS

We've all seen those videos on Facebook where a runner falls on the track and another competitor risks their winning to pick them up. Those videos touch us and there is a reason why they go viral and receive thousands of likes. They personify the best of who we are as people. Those stories show one champion supporting another when they aren't able to do it for themselves. What it proves is that a champion's heart is always bigger than their ego and they are not afraid of selfless sacrifice when necessary.

> A champion's heart is always bigger than their ego.

One of the most cited examples of sportsmanship is the story of what happened in the women's 5000 meters race in the 2016 Rio Olympics. New Zealand's Nikki Hamblin and United States' Abbey D'Agostino stumbled on the track during the semifinals heat. Despite her rigorous training for the past four years, D'Agostino took the time to check on her rival and help her up. Moments later, D'Agostino collapsed due to her injury. Hamblin then came to her side. Both finished the race well behind the other competitors. Hamblin later said, "When I look back on Rio 2016, I'm not going to remember where I finished, I'm not going to remember my time . . . but I'll always remember that moment." Times like these remind us that our most successful wins often have nothing at all to do with medals and titles.

When survey responders were asked to think of someone they viewed as a champion and describe what they did to earn that title, they reiterated the importance of being an advocate. Champions were admired for their ability to be an advocate for themselves and go after their dreams, but their legacy was marked by key moments of selfless sacrifice when necessary. Champions take care of themselves so they have the mindset, presence, and voice to show up for others in a way that is needed. They are not always giving to a point where they feel empty because then they cannot be an advocate for themselves. However, in moments that matter, champions risk their safety, success, or security to be a champion for others.

Being an advocate for someone is not forcing them out of their mess when they are not ready or putting them on your back and doing the work for them. Champions stand by the individual, grab them when they slip, and encourage them when they make progress. Champions accept that if their actions get in the way of someone being a champion for themselves then that is not loving, it is enabling and self-destructive. A champion's actions never prevent someone from being their own champion. This allows the individual to prove to themselves they have the mindset and knowledge to overcome any experience moving forward. In this space they find their resilience and self-worth. Champions would never take that gift away from anyone.

> A champion's actions never prevent someone from being their own champion.

Abraham Lincoln said, "If once you forfeit the confidence of your fellow citizens, you can never regain their respect and esteem." Being a champion for others is one of the surest ways to earn an individual's respect and keep it. You can do this by recognizing and acknowledging them for their efforts.

In a world where so many people do not feel seen, your recognition is quite often the spark that can ignite someone's potential and earn you exponential amounts of trust. Stephen R. Covey, author of the best-selling book, *The 7 Habits of Highly Effective People*, emphasizes the importance of making deposits into people's "emotional bank account." This account is not made up of money, but of trust between you and the other person. Every action you take, or don't take, is an investment or a withdrawal of trust. Champions are intentional about making deposits into other people's emotional bank accounts—without any conditions attached to their generosity. Examples of emotional deposits are being fully present and listening to the other person when they talk, sending a thank you message, acknowledging their perspective, inviting them to join you or the group you are with, helping them when they ask or don't ask for it, and recognizing them publicly or privately. Champions make emotional deposits because it is the right thing to do, it is a way to stand up for others, and it reflects their character. Additionally, champions understand they are human and they are not always going to get it right. They are going to have a bad day where they lose their cool, forget to follow through with a commitment, and not live up to someone else's expectations. Therefore, champions invest in their relationships so their account never becomes insufficient. All relationships end, and trust is eroded when one or all parties in a relationship become emotionally bankrupt. People become emotionally bankrupt in their marriage, with their boss, or with friends when they perceive the other person consistently taking more out of the relationship than they are investing. There will come a point when they are no longer willing to put up with someone's consistent overdrafts and they will walk away.

Yum! Brands (the parent company of Taco Bell, Pizza Hut, and KFC) is an organization renowned for its recognition culture. They understand the personal value and the business case for making emotional deposits, so they use public recognition to stand up for people and make them feel seen. Every leader in the organization is encouraged to have their own personalized recognition award that they can give to others. There are walls on every floor that display the recognition cards of people who have been recently recognized. There is a marching band made up of employees playing tambourines and mini hand clappers that comes around and circles someone's desk/cubical area and gives them the "culture hero" award for living the values of the organization. Perhaps even more effectively, many leaders start or end their team meetings with recognition among the group attending. This organization is creating the intentional space for people to be champions for each other, and everyone wins when that happens.

Every day is going to provide you with the opportunity to stand up for others. Sometimes it might be recognizing a stranger for their exceptional customer service. Other times it might be sending your partner or friend a text message just letting them know you are thinking of them. And in rare but pivotal moments, you might be called to stand up for someone who does not have the courage to stand up for themselves and who needs a champion. Be the champion that you would want someone to be for you!

FROM BANKRUPT TO INVESTMENT

1. Identify the relationships in your life (personal and professional) that are close to being bankrupt.

2. How have you contributed to that status?

3. What would be the value of investing back into those relationships?

4. What emotional deposits would you be willing to make this week?

ALL CHAMPIONS ARE LEADERS, BUT NOT ALL LEADERS ARE CHAMPIONS

What this research proves is that all champions are leaders, but not all leaders are champions. Leaders and champions both have competence and vision, but the difference is *how* they go about achieving that vision. Champions hold themselves accountable to how they get results, not just the results themselves. They have personal goals, but they do not sabotage other's ambitions in pursuit of their own. Champions use their influence to become the best version of themselves while lifting others up, creating opportunities for exposure, and empowering people to become their best version. In summary, champions use their influence to create a positive legacy that lives on long after they are gone.

THE POWER OF CHAMPIONS IN YOUR LIFE

Anyone who has ever done anything great did not do it on their own. They had an army of champions behind them that helped pave the way for them to be where they are. Some of your champions encouraged you when you needed it the most. Some of your champions opened doors to opportunities that gave you the exposure you needed. Some of them believed in you until you could believe in yourself. All their actions have served one defining function: to give you the courage you need to play bigger in your own life.

Sometimes, in the pursuit of your dreams, you fool yourself into believing you are all alone or you have the desire to prove to yourself that you don't need help. Please be careful that your deep need to be independent does not turn into detachment where you deflect the help of champions all around you.

Playing bigger does not typically happen in one defining moment. It is the collective power of small, meaningful moments over time, provided by champions in your life, that gives you the courage you need to stand up, show up, and speak up. In these small, meaningful moments you monumentally grow your self-confidence and give yourself permission to do it again.

Aaron Kessinger became my father figure after my dad passed away. In 2007, he called me and asked if I would consider leaving the public school classroom to teach adults in corporate America. I had never considered this before and never knew this was even an option for someone with my skill set. Aaron saw my potential and offered me an invitation to play bigger. I stepped into the opportunity he provided, and that choice fundamentally changed the trajectory

ACT LIKE A CHAMPION

of my career. It led to more developmental opportunities, networking, travel, and exposure than I ever received in public school education. He has been a constant champion in my life whose actions have opened the door to other champions I never would have met along my journey.

I deeply believe there are people who want to be your champion, just like Aaron has been for me. They want to see you succeed and share your message with the world. Sometimes they just need direction on how they can best support you. Ensure your energy invites champions in your life. Have enough humility and gratitude to receive the love they offer you. Show up and make the most of every opportunity. And, more importantly, be a champion for others. The universe will reciprocate your generosity.

WHAT TO DO IF YOU DON'T FEEL LIKE A CHAMPION

There are going to be plenty of people reading this who say, "This sounds great, but I don't feel like a champion!" I would lovingly reply, "You don't need to feel like a champion. You need to act like one." Acting like a champion is making a conscious choice to rise up—even when you do not feel like it—and applying the three behaviors of a champion anyway.

Millard Fuller, founder and former president of Habitat for Humanity International, has been quoted as saying, "It is easier to act yourself into a new way of thinking than it is to think yourself into a new way of acting." For example, sometimes owning the thought, "I am a champion" might seem disingenuous or fake to someone who doesn't believe they are. Therefore, trying to change their mindset before they change their actions can be an arduous process for everyone involved. I have coached many leaders who were emotionally disconnected and sacrificed relationships for results. Getting them to change their mindset before they change their actions does not serve them or the people around them. They can understand and rationalize how showing up different would be valuable, so we talk about actions a leader would take if they were focused on building influence through people. Afterwards, they commit to applying some of the actions in their life. Time after time, clients are successful at applying these actions, the results are positive, and so, with every little milestone they achieve,

> Do the work until your mindset catches up with the boldness of your actions.

they start to experience the benefits of a new mindset. What it proves for my clients is that their mindset is derived out of consistent, intentional actions that produce positive results. Therefore, your job is to do the work until your mindset catches up with the boldness of your actions.

So much of what it takes to be a champion happens when no one else is watching. No one gets to see all the late hours you put in while in pursuit of your dreams. No one is going to fully understand everything you had to sacrifice to get where you wanted to be. Not many people will witness your entire journey and how you had to keep picking yourself back up. Not many people are going to see all the incredible ways you stood up for others. Living your life as a champion is not always going to be comfortable or visible, but it will be meaningful.

Champions are not the result of luck or chance.

It is in life's most challenging moments that you must remind yourself you are hardwired to be a champion. Every champion fails, but they do not label themselves as failures. They make an uncomfortable choice to fail forward by refusing to give up on themselves and by finding an opportunity to learn from every situation. Champions are not the result of luck or chance. They are birthed out of a mindset, driven by vision, and cultivated from their relentless commitment to just keep going. Your life will be defined by your moments in the spotlight, but your character will be shaped under the sweat and relentless commitment when all the lights are off, when all the spectators are gone, and it is just you standing in the boldness of your dreams. It is there, in that vulnerable space, that champions are made.

Never forget: You have everything it takes to be a champion for yourself and others. Being a champion is a mindset, a choice, and it is bold. Act like a champion!

Today, I honor the fact that I was designed to be a champion who leaves a positive mark on the world. I accept that everything I've been through has provided me with the perspective and resilience I needed to be both a champion for myself and for others. This mindset emboldens me to take a stand for people and recognize them in a way that so many others might not take the time to do. Today, I will be fully present and attentive to the people around me. I will defend those who need it, and I will recognize meaningful contributions—regardless of how small they might be. I will end my day with an overwhelming sense of gratitude knowing I lived up to my potential.

CHAPTER SIX
LEADERSHIP SUMMARY

- Purpose is the unbreakable bond between you and your soul, and it is the catalyst for getting you from where you are today to where you want to be tomorrow.

- Clarity of purpose shapes how you show up and communicate as a leader. It increases your self-confidence, focus, and drive. It helps you answer the universal question, "Who am I?" and cultivate an authentic voice that builds stronger trust and connection with others.

- When you lack clarity of purpose you search endlessly for validation, you live a life others want for you, and you always play smaller than your potential.

- If you want empowering leaders at all levels of the organization then you should start by helping them understand who they are and how their personal purpose connects with the purpose of the organization.

6

want to be a great leader of yourself?

LIVE IN PURPOSE

You are amazing
Born with a unique purpose
Only you can live

In 2016, a lady pulled up to a Taco Bell drive-thru window. The restaurant's General Manager looked at the lady in the car and could tell something was wrong. She opened the window and asked the woman if she was okay. The woman paused and after talking for a moment she explained she was headed to her first chemotherapy treatment and was going alone. The manager knew there was nothing she could say to make this better for the woman, but she could show compassion. She said, "Listen, I know this might sound a little weird, but I've been told I give great hugs. Can I give you a hug before you go?" The woman opened her car door and there, between the Taco Bell drive-thru window and the car, were two women embracing each other. One using their presence to let another know she is loved and that she matters.

Living in purpose is not about changing the entire world. It is about using your presence and skills to change one person's world. Some of the most purposeful experiences in your life will happen in small, everyday moments.

You, regardless of the circumstances you were born into, were designed to live a life of purpose and fulfillment. Sometimes through life's challenges and the busyness of our day-to-day, we step out of our authentic power, bury our inner champion, and slap a big "Do Not Resuscitate" order right on our soul. With each failed relationship, the promotion we didn't receive, the loss of people we loved, the forgiveness we never granted, or the anger we never resolved, we stitch together the pain of our past, and instead of living our lives with purpose, we live as victims. As a result, we're miserable, we're searching for purpose and meaning, and we try to use external solutions to fix our internal problems. It is an empty promise, every time.

Mark Twain once said, "The two most important days of your life are the day you are born and the day you find out why." This quote reminds us that some people will spend their entire life without a clear understanding on why they do what they do, but the ones who figure it out will live a life of meaning and their success will be defined by the mark they left on this world.

Purpose is an unbreakable bond between you and your soul.

WHAT IS PURPOSE?

Purpose is an unbreakable bond between you and your soul. It is an agreement between you and the universe that you will stand for something bigger than yourself, that you will use your unique skills and experiences to help others, and that you will refuse to ever play smaller than your potential. Your purpose is a culmination of your past, talents, and lessons learned colliding to serve something bigger than yourself. It is uniquely yours and it grants you permission to take everything you've been through and make something purposeful come from it. Your pure willingness to honor a purpose you believe in will offer you the courage to step into your personal power.

Purpose is about having a vision for your life and the mark you want to make. Purpose is not something you turn on and off like a switch. It is a way of living. Your purpose is not a role. Your role just provides you the platform to live out your purpose and share your message. Purpose is not something you just do at a charity event or as a company project. Purpose is who you are. It is how you show up in the world every day. Your choices, presence, mindset, and words all serve as a North Star to how committed you are to your purpose. Leaders who live their life driven by purpose learn to have their feet planted in reality, but their heart and actions aligned with the boldness of their dreams. They use their words, their presence, and their experiences to make others feel less alone. You raise yourself to a new standard of living when you know what you stand for and why you do what you do.

Purpose gives people a reason to celebrate your legacy. We celebrate people's legacy not because they served themselves, but because they used what they had—right where they were in their journey—to serve others and make a positive mark on people's lives. They accept that their purpose transcends their education, their financial status, their race, their sexual orientation, their spirituality, and their titles. Living a life of purpose is not about changing the whole world, but it is doing what you feel called to do to change one person's world.

You have the right and freedom, at any moment, to redefine who you want to be. It is in rediscovering who you are that you unshackle yourself from the unnecessary limits you put on yourself and make a conscious choice to play bigger in your own life.

> You have the right and freedom, at any moment, to redefine who you want to be.

CELEBRATE YOUR FREEDOM MOMENTS

Elizabeth Gilbert said, "The most interesting moment of a person's life is what happens to them when all their certainties go away. Then who do you become? Then what do you look for? That's the moment when the universe is opening up an invitation."

One of my invitations came in 2016. That is the year I lost my best friend—the person who made each day brighter and who taught me how to love better. The person who had danced their way into my life, who I talked with about marriage and raising kids, decided he needed to step off the dance floor so he could find himself. With no warning and no prior conversation, this beautiful future we had created shattered into a million tiny pieces and I was left—alone—to figure out what I wanted to do with these fragile remnants. In that vulnerable space, I asked myself, "Who am I?" and, "Who do I want to be moving forward?"

You will have moments throughout your life when everything that was certain becomes uncertain and you are offered the opportunity to rediscover a bold new version of yourself. Those windows of opportunity are what I call your "Freedom Moments." Freedom moments break you open and allow you the independence to decide how you will put yourself back together and what new mindset or mission you will own.

Freedom moments are so pivotal because, for a period of time, they readjust your focus on how you see yourself, relationships, your values, what makes you happy, and why you do what you do. They grant you the ability to see the truth of your reflection. These moments do not last forever, though. If you do not lean into these feelings and discover what you can learn from them then you will miss the opportunity. You will go back to your busyness and often repeat the same patterns of behavior that got you into your mess in the first place.

Freedom moments are your invitation to find your authentic voice, to stand in your authentic confidence, and to hold yourself to a new standard of living. Freedom moments require you to answer one fundamental question: WHO AM I?

WHO AM I?

I believe one of the most challenging and vulnerable questions you will ever ask yourself is, "Who am I?" *A Course in Miracles* says, "Every decision you make stems from what you think you are and represents the value that you put upon yourself." The core of our self-worth is always rooted in what and who we believe we are. If we want to change our life and our presence we must be willing to change our belief about who we think we are.

The answer behind, "Who am I?" requires you to move past any of your titles and the things you've used to validate yourself over the years. In this vulnerable space you come face to face with your soul and you are called to align the outer image you project to the world with the inner image of how you see and feel about yourself. When we each have the courage to look at ourselves in the mirror—free of self-judgment and criticism—we allow ourselves the opportunity to see if who we are today is who we want to be tomorrow. We discover both our humanity and humility in the truth of our own reflection.

I was teaching a leadership workshop in Chicago, Illinois and helping leaders articulate why they do what they do. I asked for a volunteer and Chris raised her hand. I asked her, "Who are you?" I told her to start by saying, "I am someone who . . . " She quickly answered with, "I am someone who is a strong, loving, caring, independent, and tough lady."

I could tell by her passion there was so much more depth to her that she wasn't allowing anyone else in the room to hear. She wasn't comfortable sharing the story of who she is. When we don't know who we are, or how to authentically talk about ourselves, we will replace our authentic story with a laundry list of adjectives. These adjectives provide no depth or insight into why we show up that way. I thanked Chris for sharing, and I told her I was going to ask her to do it one more time, but this time I wanted her to think about a key experience in her life that shaped how she showed up every day—good or bad. Before having her share again, I provided her with the example of who I am.

I am someone who believes your voice and presence can change the world. I believe you might not change the whole world, but that you have the incredible power to change one person's world based on how you show up for them. I know what it is like to not show up for people, to not show up for yourself, to play smaller than your potential, and to blame everyone else so you can avoid looking at yourself in the mirror. I am someone who has done a lot of soul-searching work to better themselves, but I still have days when I question myself and beat myself up for choices I have made. I am, however, someone who has learned to give myself and others a break, to realize we are all doing the best we know how to, and to believe that we all have the power to change and honor our best self.

I could tell after the example that Chris got it! I looked back and said, "Chris . . . who are you?" Her response created palpable silence in the room and for the first time in a long time Chris allowed people to really see her. She connected in a way that other leaders recognized her for throughout the workshop.

"I am a suicide survivor. When I was 17 years old, my brother chose to take his own life. It was the most devastating thing I've ever been through. The last time I saw him alive he begged me not to leave and I chose to leave. The shame and the guilt have been horrendous. For years, I believed it was my fault he died. Over time, I've learned to not blame myself, to not take on that shame, and to pick myself up by my bootstraps. I've learned to have empathy. I've learned to be that strong, independent caring person who has a heart for everybody. I am now able to see other people's pain and their vulnerability."

When you change what you believe, you change what you see. If you want to re-experience life, you have to re-envision how you show up in it. One of the core fundamental steps in you shifting your self-perspective and developing a stronger sense of self-worth is knowing who you are—in every season of your life. You will stop fighting to be seen when you learn to love the image of who you already are.

Hold onto your sense of self, regardless of what happens to you. A lover might leave you, a boss might fire you, a friend might hurt you, but make certain to never extinguish that deep sense of knowing about who you are. It is your responsibility to protect and defend it, at all costs. You will know you are with the right people, and in the right company, when they are just as passionate about protecting and defending it as well. Greg Creed, CEO of Yum! Brands, once said to me, "If you have to give up who you are to be successful in your job then you are in the wrong job."

"WHO AM I?" EXERCISE

1. Answer the question, "Who are you?"

   a. Do not answer with any title.

   b. Start by saying, "I am someone who . . . "

   c. Go below the surface to who you really are, what you stand for, why those things are important to you, and where you learned them.

   d. Give yourself permission to talk from your heart-space versus your head-space.

WHY IS PURPOSE IMPORTANT?

Your purpose should be what inspires you to get up in the morning and say, "Yes! This is what I'm supposed to be doing." Your purpose is bigger than any one role and it pushes you to do more and learn more. Your purpose transforms your pain and teaches you how everything you've been through in your life can be used for something meaningful. Your purpose is your living reminder that you are part of something so much bigger than yourself. When you discover your purpose you stop blindly showing up for a job and you make a conscious commitment to walk in your purpose where you are happier and more engaged.

A Course in Miracles says, "Be not content with littleness [. . .] Your function is not little, and it is only by finding your function and fulfilling it that you can escape from littleness." Our littleness results from our lack of awareness. When we increase our awareness, we increase our divine possibilities.

> Purpose is the catalyst for getting you from where you are today to where you want to be tomorrow.

Purpose is the catalyst for getting you from where you are today to where you want to be tomorrow. The universal Law of Attraction states that what you focus on is what you manifest in your life. When we are intentional with both our thoughts and actions the universe supports our intentionality. Without a clear vision of who you are and why you do what you do, you will wander aimlessly through life just waiting for purpose to show itself in a sign or in a dream. Stop waiting, and create your own purpose. That deliberate action will set into motion a series of next right answers to get you closer to where you want to be.

I had the opportunity to meet an incredible woman named Rachel in 2016. Rachel and I met during a snorkeling excursion on the Big Island of Hawaii. I was sitting by myself on the boat and this woman who was full of life started asking me questions and invited me to spend time with her and her friends. Over the next several months, Rachel and I developed a close relationship and I learned more about her past and how her experiences launched her into a purpose that she lives out every day.

Rachel often felt alone and abandoned as a little girl. Her biological dad wasn't in the picture because he was in jail. Her mom remarried when Rachel was five and at age 12 she was molested by her stepdad. When this fragile little girl finally had the courage to tell her mom, her mother didn't do anything about it and continued to stay married to the man who victimized her. Rachel said, "I relied on my mom to do the right thing for her little girl, but she didn't." As a result, Rachel said she spent years wandering aimlessly through life with low self-worth, feeling angry, and allowing people into her life who should not have been there.

Rachel and I talked about purpose and she defined it as being at peace with whatever you do: the choices you make, the people you spend time with, and the boundaries you create. Rachel discussed that she deeply cares for others because she didn't have anyone care for her the way they should have or the way she needed them to. Rachel went on to say that when she had the awareness that her purpose was using her presence to make people feel less alone in the world, she gained peace, she instilled a new sense of self-worth, and it reshaped how she saw and interacted with others.

Rachel's story, along with over 200 leaders I surveyed, all aligned with three universal benefits that happen when you create purpose in your life.

BENEFIT #1: INCREASED SELF-CONFIDENCE

When you are filled with authentic purpose you stop auditioning in life because you believe you are already starring in the role of a lifetime. You stop putting your self-worth in external factors like your title, other people, your grades, or your number of followers on social media because you understand that success is an inside job.

Your purpose transforms your past pain and teaches you how everything you've been through can be used for something meaningful. Purpose pulls people out of the victim role and shows them how to transform their experiences into opportunity. This mindset turns reluctance into resilience. Find the opportunity in your experiences and you will rise up with a stronger sense of self-worth and purpose.

Purpose helps you turn reality into enough. You stop believing that you must accomplish more to be fulfilled or valuable. This doesn't mean you don't have a deep desire to fulfill goals and dreams. It simply means your self-worth is not tied to those plans.

You make the hard choice to give up on some things in life so you can lean into the things that fulfill you. You make a conscious decision to give up the person everyone else wants you to be, give up the disappointment others might have because you decided to make a bold decision to live life on your terms, and give up waking up every morning without a sense of meaning. Giving up on other people's expectations of you allows you the strength to get up and become who you were designed to be. It is in that space where you find the core of your self-confidence.

BENEFIT #2: INCREASED FOCUS

A few years ago, one of the three bulbs in my kitchen light went out. I was so busy traveling that I didn't bother to replace the bulb for months. I told myself, "I can still function. I can still see. It's not causing me any problems." When I finally decided to take action and replace it, I realized two of the three bulbs were blown. I was confused about how I did not notice this and then it reminded me of what Iyanla Vanzant says, "Your eyes adjust to the level of deficiency." Once I replaced the bulbs, I was shocked at how much more I could see and the clarity I had. I was frustrated that I would allow myself to stay in the dark when I had the resources to make the situation different. I learned that resources without awareness are futile. Awareness raises our focus and it enables us to find the necessary resources to change our situation.

When we do not have a strong sense of purpose in our lives we learn to function without it. It is our ability to function in dysfunction that often keeps us playing small. Purpose gives us the awareness we need so we can make better decisions that will pull us out of our current situation and up towards our vision.

Purpose is important because it radically shifts your vision. When you can state why you do what you do, you elevate your vision for yourself and your confidence always increases as a result. This is exactly what happened to John. John participated in one of my workshops where we help leaders articulate their purpose. After the workshop he said, "Before, I had mistakenly thought of myself as an operator who used training and development as tools for my team. Now that I know my purpose is to teach others that they are capable of greatness, it has transformed not only how I see my job, but also how I see myself. The fact is that I am, at my core, a teacher, coach and mentor who just happens to run a restaurant." He went on to talk about how a competitor offered him more money to go work for their organization. Understanding his purpose allowed him to make a better decision on how to move forward in his life. He said, "When they made it clear they had little interest in supporting my passion for growing others, I knew that was not a position I wanted within their organization, and I walked away."

Your purpose shapes the lens through which you see the world and make decisions. It grants you perspective that you never saw before and it helps you refocus when you start to veer in a direction that you intuitively know is not where you want to be. If you want to raise the quality of your life, you must raise your vision. Your vision should always be rooted in and aligned with your purpose. A lack of purpose will always keep you wandering in the dark.

BENEFIT #3: INCREASED DRIVE

Each of us is born with a spark inside. That spark represents our passion for life and people. When people say, "Never dim your light," what they are telling you is do not lose that energy and excitement you have. Our job is to nurture the spark inside us and fuel it, so it transforms into an inner flame that burns bright. That inner flame moves us from someone with passion to someone with drive. Drive trumps passion because it is action-oriented. I know a lot of passionate people who do not accomplish their goals. Why? Because transformation is created through drive, not passion.

Drive is the key ingredient to transformation because it propels you forward. You're not worried about getting it wrong. You're not worried about what others will think. Your biggest fear is doing nothing at all and not honoring that feeling inside of you that knows you are capable of more.

My best friend Chad is a passionate and talented photographer. However, it took him years before he had the drive to act on his purpose. It was not until he was laid off from his job at a small start-up company that he took the time to examine his purpose and what he wanted out of his life. Every time he talked about photography I would hear his passion. Finally, one day I just asked him, "I can tell you are passionate about photography, but you are not intentionally doing anything with your passion. What's really going on?" Chad was so overwhelmed at the process of starting, making the right choices, and being successful in the moment that his fear paralyzed him from doing anything at all. The more we talked, the more I realized that his purpose was capturing life's most meaningful moments for people and giving them something they could hold onto. We discussed actions that he would take if he were living his purpose and not afraid to get things wrong. He said, "I would have a website, and I would be building my portfolio." Today, Chad has officially launched his photography website and built a portfolio of corporate events, headshots, and special occasions. Every action he took built his confidence, and it gave him the drive to do even more. He transformed his inner spark into a flame that is burning bright and making a difference in his life and in others.

Purposeful people aren't perfect. In fact, they often take their pain, screw-ups, and mistakes and turn them into purpose. Therefore, they do not hold themselves hostage to the past. They do not keep reaching back to what was or could have been. They are focused on moving forward with intention, so they can make a difference. They have chosen to live their lives differently, hold themselves accountable to their purpose, and see where the journey takes them—until there is no more journey. It is there that their legacy will be defined.

Great leaders are not driven by possessions. Great leaders are driven by legacy. They turn their passion into drive and, as a result, they live a life of fulfillment. The driving factor? Purpose.

DANGERS OF NOT KNOWING YOUR PURPOSE

When we lose sight of who we are, we lose our voice. When we lose our voice, we lose our confidence. When we lose our confidence, we do not say the things we need to say, we do not honor our vision for our life, and we make decisions that are better for others. As a result, we wake up years later realizing we put everyone else before ourselves. This choice is not altruistic or empathetic. It is self-sabotaging and the person we really hurt is ourself.

Here are two dangers of not knowing your purpose:

DANGER #1: YOU REPLACE EMPTINESS WITH VALIDATION

Matthew Kelly, author of the book *The Rhythm of Life*, says, "in the absence of a genuine understanding of the meaning and purpose in our lives, we substitute it with shallow and superficial meaning." When we do not have authentic purpose we feel empty, so we search tirelessly for validation. We sacrifice ourselves and our values for anything that will make us feel "good enough." As a result, we become addicted to whatever fuels our validation.

I coached a client who was a self-proclaimed "validation junkie." He was brought up to believe success was about external factors like career and education. He was always on a quest to do more and be more. When he did not receive the validation fix he wanted, or his short-term fix wore off, he would get angry, blame others, and start his quest for validation all over again. He acknowledged throughout our coaching that, "I have never given myself permission to just be okay with what I've done, who I am, and where I am in my life." He accepted that he had lived a lot of his life in fear of not being good enough. He slowly started to find ways to turn his fear into his purpose, so he could give himself the validation he needed versus manipulating and using other people for it. He realized it was not money or a title he was searching for. It was purpose.

When we do not know who we are or what we stand for, we search endlessly for external factors to make us feel worthy. Emptiness makes us feel alone and, when we feel alone, we fight to be seen. When we do not feel seen, we gravitate to whatever takes away the pain and makes us feel connected. These external factors put a temporary Band-Aid over our emptiness, but the moment the Band-Aid comes off we use our partners, kids, friends, boss, and even strangers to take away our pain. We exhaust others and erode the relationships that mean the most to us in our campaign for validation.

DANGER #2: YOU LIVE THE LIFE OTHER PEOPLE WANT FOR YOU

It's hard to know who you are when you don't even tell yourself the truth. When you do not know who you are or what you stand for, you buy into other people's interpretations and expectations of who they want you to be. You end up putting on masks everywhere you go in life so you can live up to those expectations. Don Miguel Ruiz explained the dangerous consequence of this behavior in his book *The Mastery of Love*. He states, "We practice and practice, and we master how to be what we are not." The irony of this is you fight so hard to "be seen," but you never even let people see the real you. Conformity does not feel good, but you spend your entire life yielding to other people's expectations to avoid disappointing them. The truth is, the person you disappoint the most is yourself.

You allow other people to manage your choices for you when you do not have a clear vision of your purpose. Sometimes these people have good intentions and are genuinely trying to help you, but because you could not articulate your purpose they give you opinions and suggestions based on their experience. Their experience is not rooted in your best interests. When you don't have a vision for your career, you will put more weight on other's ideas for your career than your own. When you don't have a vision for your relationship, you will allow your partner to decide what's in the best interests of both people. When you don't have a vision of your core values, your sacrifice yours for other people's.

Your vision for your life and the mark you want to leave helps you make decisions; therefore, when you have no filter on how to make choices you take people up on their suggestions and then wake up years later feeling stuck, wishing you had made some different choices earlier on, or applying for every job that becomes available.

Refuse to live a life that other people want for you. Do not get so caught up living the life you want that you do not enjoy and honor the one you already have. Your life is your choice, and living a life of purpose is one of the most important decisions you will ever make.

HOW TO DISCOVER YOUR AUTHENTIC PURPOSE

It is no one else's responsibility to help you create a vision for your life. If you want to find your purpose, you must start by honoring your past. Your purpose is always rooted in your past and it is a direct reflection of every experience you've been through—both good and bad. Your past does not have to define where you are going, but—do not be mistaken—it has shaped who you are and how you lead, love, and communicate.

If you want to play to the level of your potential, you must create a vision for your life. The beautiful part is that you don't have to get your vision "right," but you must get it clear. With clarity comes action, and all action will lead you to your next right answer.

DOWNLOAD FREE "DISCOVER YOUR PURPOSE" HANDOUT
Download an electronic copy of this handout at boldnewyou.com

Step 1: Influential People

- List the *people* in your life—both good and bad—who have shaped you.

- Next to their name or initials, highlight the lesson they taught you about life, yourself, etc.

- Identify a minimum of 7-10 influential people.

Step 2: Key Experiences

- List the *experiences* in your life—both good and bad—that have shaped you.

- Next to the experience, highlight the lesson you learned from it.

- Identify a minimum of 7-10 key experiences.

Step 3: Polaroid Picture

- Imagine you had to summarize your entire life up to this point in one Polaroid picture.

- What is the feeling and / or image you would see on that picture?

- Briefly explain why.

Step 4: Identify Your Theme

- Take a few moments to review all the *lessons* you wrote down.

- You should notice a recurring theme in your life.

- Write down the theme(s) that had a big impact on your life.

Examples of themes are the following:
love, fear, faith, family, power of words, hope, resilience, overcomer, courage, second chances, reinvention, brokenness, lack of confidence, uncertainty, loneliness, emotionally disconnected, security, forgiveness, risk, trust, silence, teaching, warrior, strength, connection, perseverance

Part 5: Purpose Formula

Now, let's take the theme of your life and turn it into your purpose. You will use the following formula to articulate your authentic purpose statement to others:

HOW + WHO + IMPACT

HOW

- Your purpose statement should start with a verb—an action word that clearly highlights how you will live out your purpose.

Examples might include the following:
teach, help, motivate, empower, give, ignite, transform, inspire, provide, change, reinvent, connect, create, build, encourage

WHO

- This part of the formula identifies the audience you want to specifically help as you live your purpose.

- When I work with leaders on this exercise I have them all just list "people" for this section because I believe purpose is a way of living and that we don't turn it on and off for specific groups of people.

- However, some individuals might want to identify a specific audience when talking about their purpose in a job interview or when marketing their business.

Examples might include the following:
teens, women, men, leaders, single moms, recovering addicts, mothers who have lost children

IMPACT

- This is where you take the theme you identified earlier and state the impact or mark you want to make.

- For example, if someone's theme is "strength", they will think about what they want to teach people about strength. They might say, "I want to teach people how to be strong regardless of what they go through." They might say, "I want to empower people to find their inner strength", or, "I want to motivate people to be a champion in their own life."

- Once you are clear on the impact you want to make because of the theme in your life, it will be easy to put together a statement you believe in.

Using the following formula, write an authentic purpose statement that you believe in.

HOW + WHO + IMPACT

15 Examples of Authentic Purpose Statements from other Leaders:

1. Teach people how to discover a bold new version of themselves.

2. Change the world one conversation at a time.

3. Empower people to make their voice and presence matter.

4. Transform how people see themselves and what they are capable of achieving.

5. Inspire people to never settle for a second-rate version of themselves.

6. Help people kick fear's ass.

7. Reinvent people's idea of failure and success.

8. Help people find the image and style that makes them stand out for all the right reasons.

9. Build people's self-worth so they never play smaller than their potential.

10. Ignite leaders' abilities to lead with both their head and heart.

11. Help people learn how to persevere through chaos.

12. Help people see the world through someone else's eyes.

13. Ignite people's fire that was once put out.

14. Teach people to reconnect to the best part of who they already are.

15. Motivate people to forgive and move forward.

Part 6: LIVE IT OUT LOUD!

How willing are you to disrupt your current pattern today so you can achieve everything you say you want tomorrow? It is one thing to know and articulate your purpose. It is another to have the courage and tenacity to live it out, unapologetically. Moving from a vision to a mission requires you to take intentional daily actions to accomplish your goal. You don't always have to know how you are going to do it, but you must do something to move forward. Your step forward is a signal to the universe that you are in this together and you are willing to do your part. People cannot support a vision they do not know.

- Outline ways you currently do and/or can live that purpose statement out in the future.

- Outline how your strengths contribute to your ability to live out that purpose.

- Articulate how your current job/role allows you to live out your identified purpose.

- What do you need to change or give yourself permission to do differently so you can live your purpose?

SHARE YOUR PURPOSE STATEMENT ON SOCIAL MEDIA

1. Write your purpose statement on your hand or on a piece of paper/sticky note. Get creative.

2. Take a picture of your authentic purpose (do a selfie if you are feeling really vulnerable and brave).

3. Post on social media using the hashtag: #BoldNewMe

NO TURNING BACK!

It is only in your belief of who you are that you can change what you are today. Who you are was perfect from the day you were born, but maybe some of your choices along your journey haven't aligned with your belief about yourself. Maybe you lost sight of who you are at the core, so you have defined who you are with titles and accolades. That's okay. These were your reactions to what happened, and you did the best you knew how—regardless of the consequences.

However, you are the architect of your life and your life is a product of your choices. When you accept that your power always lies in your choices then you automatically grant yourself permission to play bigger. It is a choice to live a life with purpose. It is a choice to get up every day and work towards something bigger than yourself, something that feeds your soul, and something that makes a mark on the world. You were not designed to play small. When you wake up every day driven by purpose you are more engaged, you walk with a new-found level of confidence, and you make your choices with stronger clarity. You become a demonstration for others on authentic empowerment when you know who you are, what you stand for, and why you do what you do. Everyone benefits when you take the necessary time to know who you are.

Mark Twain's quote at the beginning of this chapter reminds us that it's not about what we do, but why we do what we do. Every day offers you a choice to live in the possibilities of your purpose, and living your purpose requires intentional commitment. The moment you rise up with a sense of purpose—a sense that you are working towards something bigger than yourself—you change the trajectory of your life and the impact that you make on the world. The moment you elevate your purpose, you elevate your life—and that will always prevent you from playing small.

Remember: some people will stumble into their purpose; some will fall into it; some will catapult themselves into their future. It doesn't matter how you discover your purpose and who you are, as long as you do.

PURPOSE AFFIRMATION

I am no accident. Every success and struggle I have been through has offered me the chance to show up better. Every failed relationship, job, and dream is part of my magnificent story that is leading me to an even better ending. I have been gifted experiences and lessons that only I can tell, and I believe someone needs to hear my story in the way only I can tell it. I accept that my purpose is so much bigger than me, and I will not turn my back on my potential. I will not sit here and rot among the waiting. I make my future. I honor that I am the only one in the world that can fulfill my purpose, and the universe needs what I have to offer. I am ready. I am prepared. I will live my purpose out loud.

BOLD NEW YOU

FROM MY DAD TO YOU

If no one tells you
They believe in you today,
I believe in you. . .

It has been 20 years since my dad passed away and since I began my journey of self-discovery. I often wonder what my dad would look like now, what advice he would have given me over the years, how he would have grown in his perspective, and what he would have been most proud of in his children. Well, I know what he would not have been proud of, and that is my inability to fix things. I recently had to call the garage door company when I found myself trapped inside the garage because the spring broke and I couldn't figure out how to manually lift up the door. Bless my heart! That's my life, y'all. Though it is funny now, moments like those make me miss my dad and all the things I admired about him. I believe if my dad were still alive, he would look at me and tell me that above everything I've accomplished, he is most proud of me for not giving up on myself—regardless of what I experienced—and that I went boldly in the direction of my dreams.

This wisdom is a reminder that your greatness will never be about what you acquire or achieve, but about who you become in the process of working towards your goals. I hope this book has helped you cultivate both the confidence and courage to be a better leader of yourself and to go boldly in the direction of your dreams. I said at the beginning that I wanted this book to help you become more of who you are at your best, and I believe at your best you are already a great leader. Sometimes we just need the reminder and other times we just need someone to hold up the mirror for us! Thank you for allowing me to be a part of your journey.

The end of this book is just the beginning of discovering a bold new version of yourself. You are just getting started and I am standing at the starting line cheering you on as you begin this incredible journey. The journey will not always go smoothly, and that's when you know you are learning. Some days you are going to get it right. Some days you are going to screw it up. That's okay! If you don't mess it up, find yourself lost, and get frustrated from time to time then you are not pushing yourself hard enough. Transformation is a messy, experiential process. You will often need to walk a mile into your future before it will all make sense.

> You will often need to walk a mile into your future before it will all make sense.

Hang on to the people you love when the journey becomes hard, but give each other enough space to grow to your highest, fullest potential. The best leaders are both the student and the teacher. Teach others what you learn. Help them see their worth so they can honor their potential. Listen, empathize, and be the student so you can receive the messages you also need to hear in your life. Don't get so caught up in being where you want to be tomorrow because someone needs you right where you are today. Above all else, please remember: your power always lies in your choices, and you always reserve the right to make a different choice.

> Your power always lies in your choices, and you always reserve the right to make a different choice.

There is a beautiful verse in the song "Saturn" by the band Sleeping at Last that says, "With shortness of breath I'll explain the infinite. How rare and beautiful it truly is that we exist." I believe, at the end of our life, the years we lived will feel like seconds. All the pain we experienced will melt away and we will only remember the people who loved us, the people we were honored to love, and the mark we made on this world. Life is short and fragile, and it is constantly whispering, "You are not designed to play small." Everything you see, hear and touch is there to remind you of your potential: from the vastness of the ocean, the grandeur of the mountains, the recognition of a job well done, the heartache of disappointment and unfulfilled expectations, to the opportunities you have yet to experience. You are a miracle in this world and you are meant to lead. Lead boldly!

From my dad to you: Life is short. Never give up on yourself no matter what happens, and just keep moving forward in the direction of your dreams. You are worth that choice.

IT IS TIME FOR A BOLD NEW YOU!

So if no one tells you they believe in you, I believe in you. Go make your mark!

ACKNOWLEDGMENTS

TRIBE

Special thanks to everyone who completed surveys, participated in interviews, provided support and insight on social media, and contributed to this book over the years. I am forever grateful for you and your time.

TACO BELL

Thank you to my Taco Bell family. You provided me with the platform and encouragement to start my own business in a time of uncertainty. I would not be where I am without you, your support, and your partnership. There will never be enough words to express my appreciation for all you have provided me with over the years. Thank you for making a mark in my life. I will do my best to pass that on and empower others to "Live Más."

US CHAMBER OF COMMERCE

Thank you for seeing value in what I teach and allowing me to be a faculty member for the Institute for Organization Management (IOM). Thank you to all the chamber and association leaders who have participated in my classes, shared their insights, and allowed me to be part of their journey.

NATIONAL COLLEGIATE ATHLETIC ASSOCIATION (NCAA)

D2 athletics — you rock!!! You brought me in years ago to work with coaches, student athletes, and administrators, and you never let me go. I would not want it any other way. You have become part of my family and I cannot wait to see the difference we make together in the future.

FRIENDS

You are the champions that pushed me to dream bigger, challenged me when I needed it, had my back when I fell, and put up with me constantly asking you for feedback. Thank you for supporting my dreams and loving me unconditionally.

Ashley Anderson
Robert Bertram
Chad Bock
Rebecca Bolte
JaneAnn Bradley
Mike Capiro
Ali Crane
David Emery
Pei-Wen Fu
Aaron Kessinger
Martin Mendelson
Jeff Nally
Sandra Ponce
Jenna Reese
Brandon Rowan
Lino Villafone

AUTHORS

Your work inspired me and gave me the space to re-imagine who I could be and what I could do in this world. Thank you!

Oprah Winfrey for introducing me to a bigger, more loving world
Iyanla Vanzant for inspiring me to be a teacher and coach
Brené Brown, *The Gifts of Imperfection*, et al.
Louise Hay, *You Can Heal Your Life*
Scott Stabile, *Big Love*
Don Miguel Ruiz, *The Mastery of Love*
Dr. Mark Goulston, *Just Listen*
Janine Driver, *You Say More Than You Think*
Vicki Halsey, *Brilliance by Design*
Simon Sinek, *Start With Why*
Marianne Williamson, *A Return to Love*
Gary Zukav, *The Seat of the Soul*

ABOUT THE AUTHOR

Justin Patton is an international speaker, author, and Executive Coach whose mission is to empower leaders to make their voice and presence matter.

From the painful death of his father to being emotionally disconnected for over 12 years, Justin understands the unintentional damage you do to your relationships, career, confidence, and leadership brand when you do not take responsibility for how you show up in the world.

Justin is the author of *Bold New You* and the upcoming book series, *Unleashing Potential*. When he is not speaking to audiences across the world or writing inspirational haikus for his social media followers, he is traveling or spending time at his home in Louisville, Kentucky.

Justin's high-energy style, relatable storytelling, and relevant messages are what make him a sought-after keynote speaker. His clients include Taco Bell, General Electric, National Collegiate Athletic Association (NCAA), Humana, US Chamber of Commerce, American Health Care Association, Energetic Women, Spear Education, The Coffee Bean & Tea Leaf, Miss Kentucky Scholarship Organization, Sky Ridge Medical, KBP Foods, and Chambers of Commerce organizations across the country.

Justin earned a master's degree in education from the University of Louisville and taught high school English in the public school system before teaching in corporate America and then starting his own company. Justin is currently a faculty member for the US Chamber of Commerce, has expertise in body language, executive presence, and emotional intelligence. Additionally, he is a member of the International Coach Federation and National Speakers Association.

For more information about Justin and his work, visit justinpatton.com.

Made in the USA
Lexington, KY
24 November 2019